REFLECTIONS OF AN
ENTREPRENEUR

RANDY ROMACK

Copyright © 2016 by Randy Romack. All rights reserved. No part of this book may be reproduced in any form, or by any means, electronic or mechanical, including photocopying, recording or by any information storage and retrieval system without express permission of the copyright owner.

Randy Romack
Palm Desert, California
E-mail: ahdcook@yahoo.com

This is a work of non-fiction

Library of Congress Cataloging in Publication
Romack, Randy
Reflections of an Entrepreneur

Printed in the United States
Reflections of an Entrepreneur / by Randy Romack

NON-FICTION/AUTO BIOGRAPHY

ISBN 13: 978-1535194044

Cover and Interior by Ron Sharrow

DEDICATION

To my mother with beautiful memories of the fabulous woman she was. Her excitement for each day, exuberance for life, humor, boundless energy, and love of people was a tremendous example. Her unconditional love of her children and wonderful spirit has always been with me and helped carry me through the toughest of times.

I LOVE YOU MOM

CONTENTS

Prologue		i
Chapter 1	Indiana	1
Chapter 2	Bean Pickers	9
Chapter 3	Asses & Elbows	13
Chapter 4	Sorry!…Mr. Defabis	19
Chapter 5	Frank & Mary	30
Chapter 6	Factory Life	35
Chapter 7	Go West Young Man	45
Chapter 8	Partners	50
Chapter 9	K-Bobs & Cabbage Rolls	57
Chapter 10	Happy Thanksgiving	63
Chapter 11	Yes…We Do	70
Chapter 12	Holy Pastrami	76
Chapter 13	Abalone for Sale	81
Chapter 14	California Dreamin'	87
Chapter 15	Meat Market for Sale	97
Chapter 16	Pizza	104
Chapter 17	Pancho	110
Chapter 18	A Big Burden	118
Chapter 19	Really in a Pickle	127
Chapter 20	Can I Go To Work With	131
Chapter 21	Mountain Escape	139
Epilogue		149
About the Author		151
Acknowledgements		152

*Enjoy the little things,
for one day you'll look back and realize
they were the big things*

~Robert Brautt

PROLOGUE

Everyone remembers being asked as kid, by a relative or some other adult, "And what do you want to be when you grow up?" Most kids never give it a thought until someone asks. The usual responses are, a fireman…policeman…airplane pilot or a cowboy… maybe an Indian Chief. As amazing as it seems, though, some know they want to be doctors, lawyers, nurses or follow in their father's footsteps and clearly pursue those dreams.

Many graduate from high school and choose college or land a job and start a thirty or forty year grind to succeed. I was among the vast number who had no clue what I was going to do with the rest of my life. College held no real promise for me; suppose I went and spent four years studying nothing in particular and still didn't know what I wanted to do, or found out I didn't like whatever I might have decided to study…then what?

Frankly, it was quite scary to think about making such a major decision. I definitely felt the pressure. Was it unrealistic to expect to find work that I might actually enjoy?

The last thing I would have ever thought of becoming was an *entrepreneur*. Hell, I had no clue what one of those was and I still stumble over that fancy word when I say it.

In reflection of my early years there were events and people who crossed my path that clearly influenced me. Maybe it was destiny that led me to become one of those entrepreneurial types. Obviously, at that time, I couldn't have imagined how important those people and circumstances were and the role they played in my life. I certainly would have paid a whole lot more attention, had I known. In a strange way, those people and events prepared me for what lay ahead.

In my case, with virtually no financial resources, I realize that pure dumb luck was responsible to a great extent for the successes I eventually achieved. I've heard it said, that you make your own luck…you just have to recognize and take advantage of it. In my case, that included the *dumb luck*! There were a bunch of *make it or break it* moments along the highway to success.

Without being overly dramatic and for whatever it may be worth…here's my story.

CHAPTER 1

INDIANA

Being raised in Indianapolis, Indiana was the best! It was an uncomplicated time, but full of adventure. I had a pretty good childhood. The first 14 years were spent in the city with little to worry about, except going to school and hanging around with my friends.

My best friend was Charlie Hilton. I don't remember exactly when we met, but we had to be really young. One thing for sure, we were pretty much joined at the hip the first 10 or 12 years of our childhood. From the moment we woke up, we would head over to one another's house and spend the day roaming around the streets and alleys of Indianapolis searching for something to entertain us. I still recall that Charlie taught me how to tie my shoes, so I would say that we certainly went back pretty far.

Charlie's dad, George, was a tall, muscular, rather good looking man. He had a ready smile that inadvertently showed his gold tooth. He always wore a fedora. It gave him a real classy Humphrey Bogart look and he wore it from dawn to dusk. I was surprised to see that he was bald when I saw him lying on their sofa taking a nap one day. I thought he actually looked good without his hat, but what does a little kid know.

The family owned a corner grocery store on Deloss Street, just a short distance from my house. It was a typical little neighborhood store with just the basics; milk, canned goods, lunch meats, cheeses, fresh cut meats, dry goods, and whatever else one might expect to find in the corner grocery store.

A long white enamel metal rack ran down the middle loaded with fresh Colonial bread products, Chesty potato chips and various tasty wrapped sweets stacked high. A long refrigerated case of fresh produce ran along another wall. Hilton's Market was always bursting at the seams and well stocked with merchandise. I remember it had a distinctively good smell. George and his wife Deck ran the store with no employees. Charlie was the youngest of their four boys, so there was never a dull moment at Charlie's house. Deck was a short woman with a beautiful, radiant face and even at that age I could imagine how stunning she must have been as a young lady. She was totally dedicated to George and the boys.

Deckter May, as George would lovingly call her, took care of the money end of the operation and would carry the zippered leather bag of cash back and forth from the store to the house. A loose credit system was in place where you could purchase items and put them on your bill. The *bill* was a bluebook for each customer with their name on the cover. It was kept under the counter. When a purchase was, made George or Deck would merely write down the date, item and amount and hopefully at the end of the week when the customer received their paycheck they would settle up the bill with the store.

On many occasions, I would be sent to the store by my mom to get an item or two and tell Deck to put it on the bill. Even at that young age, I remember thinking the Hilton's had a pretty neat life, running their grocery store and living next door. They could eat whatever they wanted, including one of Deck's famous super rich, chocolate pies or any dinner request shouted out by the boys.

Speaking of eating whatever one wanted, once in a while, Charlie would be asked to cover the store for an hour or two while his parents ran errands. I relished those times because, as Charlie's constant companion, I would help him *watch the store*. At the most, five minutes after his mom and dad left Charlie would ask me if I was hungry...well, what a question to ask a kid standing next to a rack loaded with Hostess Twinkie's, chocolate cupcakes, pastries and various other tasty sugary morsels, not to mention a candy display brimming with Snicker Bars, Clark Bars and Hershey Bars and Jujubes.

I was a rather skinny kid raised on healthy, wholesome meals my mom would prepare from scratch. My dad was quite the gardener, so there was a steady menu of healthy dishes constantly served in our house. We rarely had sweets or candy around the house, so the irresistible display at Hilton's made my mouth water.

I had to constrain myself to sheepishly answer Charlie's hunger question with a hesitant, "Well *maybe* I am a *little bit* hungry." Then, while Charlie was waiting on customers, I would proceed to stuff as many Twinkie's, Snicker Bars and deep fried cherry pies down my throat as I could swallow. I had no thought whatsoever of the Hilton's profit and loss statement. Another part of the treat was digging into the ice cream section and swallowing as many drumsticks and cream sickles I could swallow before his mom returned.

I did feeling a little bit guilty when Mrs. Hilton would thank me for *helping* Charlie, *watch the store.* Shortly after this gluttony episode, I would have to go home and sit down to a nice wholesome meal my mom had prepared. I would take a few bites; wait for my mom to leave the room for a minute and scrape most of the food on my plate in the trash to avoid her getting upset because I did not eat what she had lovingly prepared.

My next work experience occurred when I was about 11 years old and I got a job shining shoes at the corner barber shop. I don't remember much about it other than it was on Saturdays and most every nickel I made was put into the pinball machine next door at the little coffee shop that specialized in chili and hamburgers. It was a pretty nice refuge on a cold Indiana day. I can still smell the hamburgers and onions cooking on the flattop grill as I swung the door open and came in from the cold. For some odd reason, I remember the jukebox playing the song *King Creole* being belted out by Elvis Presley.

During the time I was honing my skills as a shoe shine boy, I dreamed of my ultimate career desire to become a newspaper delivery boy for one of the three Indianapolis dailies. The only thing that kept me from achieving this lofty goal was the fact that I was 11 years old and I needed to be 13 before I would be considered for a job as a *carrier.*

What to do? Well I had the bright idea of getting my birth certificate from my mother's box of important documents and *expertly* change my birth year by two years. My hands trembled as I *cleverly* erased my birth year from the beautiful fancy scripted document from St. Vincent's Hospital. I carefully took a pen and inserted the birth year of my dreams. My next step was to go to the regional newspaper office to see Big Ed about the prospects of my future employment. I don't know if Ed was desperate for carriers or if I caught him in the right mood, but he accepted my *perfectly forged document* as conclusive proof that I was, indeed, 13 years old.

To my utter amazement I became a carrier for the Indianapolis News. My 87 customers were on Walcott Street., where I lived and Randolph Street, the next street over. Every day after school and on Saturdays I would go by the paper distribution hut and pick up my *hot off the press* copies of the News. I would hastily hand roll the newspapers into a tight roll, stuff them in my canvas bags, put the bags over my bicycle handlebars and rode my route.

I pedaled at *supersonic* speed, accurately throwing the evening edition on the customer's porch as I balanced on my Schwinn Red Phantom. At the end of the week, it was my job to knock on each customer's door and collect for the delivered papers. That was my first exposure to the realities of being self-employed. Every Saturday, Mr. Setters wanted to be paid for the newspapers. What was left after I paid him was my profit. Well, since my route was located in a middle class area, the people did not always answer the door to pay me or they would otherwise avoid me. So I found myself having to hound people to collect my money, which would often times take four or five weeks to collect what represented my profit.

That was a harsh lesson for me in Business Reality #1; the

boss is the last one in the food chain to eat! I did manage to collect on most of those deadbeats and was able to whittle out a small profit. The profits themselves were invested in the local ice cream parlor or White Castle hamburgers.

The newspaper was always pressuring the carriers to get new customers and held contests to motivate us to knock on doors for *starts* as they referred to new subscribers. I vividly remember a Yo Yo promotion they conducted where a Japanese Yo Yo master came to the station and did all these wonderful tricks with a Yo Yo. He showed off the *walk the dog*, *around the world* and *rocking the cradle* using the Duncan Super Tournament Pro Yo Yo that I could have for free by signing up only ten new customers. I was totally motivated. Wow! It worked…I got one.

The most memorable promotion, was pounding on countless doors to win a trip to Fort Knox, Kentucky. I recall having had to get thirty new starts to win. I got the last new subscriber just in the final closing hour by promising to mow their lawn for free. So the next week it was off to the Fort Knox army base with a bus load of screaming newspaper boys. The experience was fun and we even were yelled at in the middle of the night by a real army sergeant for not shutting up and going to sleep. The next day was filled with riding around in army tanks, eating at a mess hall and watching flame throwers in action. Pretty neat stuff for an ~~11~~ 13 year old kid.

Every state has its traditions. In Indianapolis, Indiana every Memorial Day weekend, the whole town went crazy for the 500 mile race. People came from all over to see this famous race. The newspaper even printed extra editions to keep up with the demand. The pre-race festivities had a tradition of the Hoosier state song, *Back Home Again in Indiana* being sung just before the race. Even today as I hear those words it makes my eyes water as I think about Indiana. After the song the command to *start your engines* was given and all thirty three cars fired up their engines to a deafening roar. That was and still is quite a spectacle. When the race winner crossed the finish line the Star Newspaper would quickly print a special edition with the winner blasted over the entire front page. It was remarkable how the freshly printed souvenir edition would be dropped off at designated corners for the carriers to pick up before the ink was completely dry. We went around hawking the papers as the cars filled the streets heading home from the track. It was quite the feat for the newspaper to pull that off with such precision. I sold those Special Editions on the corner of Walcott St. and Southeastern Ave. and did a great job for a kid. I still remember the headlines that year, **SAM HANKS WINS 500.**

I advanced to a dream route of the Indianapolis Star morning edition, which required me to jump out of bed at 4:30 a.m. It was a tough assignment, especially during the cold Indiana winters. It was a family joke about how I went to bed early, fell asleep then woke up an hour later and ran downstairs , fully clothed thinking I was late for my route. Everyone was sitting in the living room watching TV and laughing.

It truly did teach me responsibility and seeing a job through till it was completed. I owe a debt of gratitude to my dad for the times he woke up on snowy, below zero mornings and drove me around on my deliveries. I think my paper delivery job helped set a foundation for my future in a small business…but why get philosophical.

My next venture into the work force came at the ripe age of ~~13~~ 15. Shortly after we moved to the small country town of Brownsburg, Indiana, just thirty miles from Indianapolis, I decided it was time for me to get more serious about earning my own money. I needed a real job. Small town Indiana did not offer many jobs outside of harvesting hay and other crops in the summer. August was the month that offered the greatest employment opportunities and that coincided with the highest hay fever pollen count. My allergies went crazy and made life unbearable.

CHAPTER 2

BEAN PICKERS

It was my lucky day when I met Montie Heath. In one's journey through life, it is rare to meet someone who remains a friend for the rest of your life. Montie was one of those lifelong friends. We shared the same dilemma of moving as young teenagers into a new town and a new school. We went to large schools with several thousand students in Indianapolis. We were uprooted and moved to Brownsburg which had only three or four hundred students in the entire school. Being uprooted as a teenager is difficult enough, but trying to adjust and blend in, proved to be quite a cultural shock.

One thing we had in common was our love of basketball. Indiana was basketball crazy. We played most every day. In winter we would shovel the snow off the court to play. When summer rolled around we decided we should maybe find something else to do instead of playing basketball all day.

We decided to get jobs and earn a little spending money. That sounded like a good idea! We had seen a sign on a bulletin board that read, "Earn cash...pick beans." There was a phone number. Montie and I looked at each other, shrugged our shoulders and said, "How hard can that be? And just like that decided, "Let's do it!" We had no car, so the old farmer agreed to pick us up in town the following morning. All right! We got the job. Sure enough, the next morning Farmer Fred, his skin like leather, and sporting his worn bib overalls, straw hat slowly drove up to the corner in a big green Buick Roadmaster. It was one of those hot August Indiana summer days when the humidity was punishing.

He wasn't about to set any speed records driving. He was clutching the steering wheel with unsteady hands and sped down the highway every bit of 15 miles an hour, as we crept out to his beloved bean patch. Montie and I were cracking jokes about him going too fast and asking if he had any air conditioning in his big Buick? He said, "Roll that window down boys, for air conditioning."

We left the Highway 136, the main road, onto a gravel road...dust was flying in the windows even at 15 miles an hour. We discovered there was a reason farmer Fred was going so slowly. Besides his shaky hands, he couldn't see! His head was bent over the giant steering wheel and it was a challenge for him to keep the big Roadmaster from weaving from side to side all over the road. He finally pulled off the gravel road to a dirt road out in the middle of nowhere.

We had arrived in a field of row after row of green beans, sprouting in all their glory. Fred explained he would pay us fifty cents for each half bushel we picked. He went on in great detail to show us how to pick the beans correctly. Okay, we got it! He gave us a jug of water and said he would be back in a few hours with lunch. We had our transistor radio with us, so we flipped it on, as he sped out of sight, a bit slower...maybe 5 miles an hour, leaving behind a small cloud of dust.

We were ready to go to work. We removed our shirts to work on our tans. The music was blaring, "In the jungle, the mighty jungle, the lion sleeps tonight." We sang along and started our bean picking venture...we were finally going to make some money. I don't know if you have ever done any farm work and picking beans in particular, but, let me tell you...it ain't easy! The first half hour was no problem. We bent over and started picking. We had filled a couple baskets, but the Indiana sun was blazing down, bugs were buzzing around and the humidity was off the charts. To make matters worse, the radio battery was nearly drained and the music was getting lower and lower.

We kept up the good humor, horsing around and throwing beans at each other. Then, the pain hit us. At that age, laziness, attention span or both could have been contributing factors, but after being bent over for a long stretch, the lower pain back hit us hard. We were guzzling the cold water, as we sat under a shade tree complaining. We made a decision to head back to town. The problem was that Fred was not coming back for a few hours...the way he drove, he might not have made it back at all. We just laughed at the thought As a confirmation of our immaturity and what we thought was a terrific joke, we took the large stacks of empty baskets and started hanging them one by one all over the big oak tree, as if we were decorating a Christmas tree. We really didn't give much thought to how we were going to get home.

As we started walking down that hot country road on our way back to town, I was sure of one thing, we could eliminate *farm hand* from our list of career choices.

CHAPTER 3

ASSES & ELBOWS

I scouted out employment opportunities and set my sights on one of the largest employers in town. Off I went to the local Saunder's IGA Food Liner and applied for a job as a shelf stocker or bag boy, or anything. Well again, I had to prove that I was older than I really was…16 this time. Luck was with me when I presented my *perfectly forged* birth certificate. Millie, the older redheaded office clerk took a look at my certificate as I was hastily telling her it was my dream to work at the IGA and how hard I would work. She gave me a wink and okayed my birth certificate that truly proved I was, indeed, 16 years old.

My time at the IGA was exciting, because I was assigned a variety of different jobs. From bagging groceries to stocking shelves, I did most everything under the watchful eye of Leroy the store manager and *whip* for Mr. Saunders, the owner. Leroy was a tall, muscular 40 or 50 year old man. He whirled around the store like a Dervish doing his best to impress Mr. Saunders so he would keep his job in a small town where there were not a lot of job opportunities.

Every Wednesday, a semi-trailer arrived loaded with boxed groceries. The challenge was always screamed out by Leroy to get the truck unloaded in record time. A few expletives were thrown into the barked orders. One of his favorite expressions was, "All I want to see is asses and elbows," as we sweated away throwing case after case of groceries from the truck onto the conveyor belt.

My ~~15~~, I mean 16 year-old body, at 135 pounds and 6'1", was not built for too much physical labor. I did manage to perform well enough in spurts; at least when Leroy cast his evil eye my way. It was always a welcomed treat when Leroy called for a smoke break and the smokers filed out the back door for a 10 minute smoke-a-thon. I would collapse on the empty cardboard boxes to re-energize until they returned.

The next phase of the Wednesday restock was to take all the boxes we unloaded and cut the tops of the cardboard off to price the cans inside. This was done with a razor sharp box cutter. I was amazed at how fast Leroy could remove a box top in one fluid motion with his cutter. The next step was to look up the price of the item and adjust the band of numbers on an adjustable rubber stamp to the proper price and rapidly price each can. Once again, Leroy was an All-American, pricing am entire carton of cans in the blink of an eye. With hundreds of boxes of cans to be priced, speed was essential if to keep Leroy from pouncing in a heartbeat. This was in pre-historic times before barcodes eliminated that job.

That was actually my first business exposure to production, taking orders and learning to get a job done with speed and efficiency.

If I wanted to keep my prized job at IGA I realized I had better get with it. I took my coveted box cutter everywhere and practiced cutting empty boxes at every opportunity. Soon I became proficient enough to get scheduled every Wednesday to help unload the truck. It got to the point where I made a game of it and found the possibility of building my skinny frame up through this *weight lifting* challenge. The camaraderie and the teamwork involved were also gratifying and I finally realized that Leroy was a good guy; he was just all bark and no bite.

I often wonder what ever became of Leroy and think about how hard his life must have been as a stocker laboring at a below-average wage. But, I didn't have time to ponder those things back then, I was focused on racking up as many work hours as possible at 73¢ per hour, than I was on figuring out the business world.

My next IGA adventure involved putting on a heavy coat and restocking the dairy and frozen food refrigerators. This was a cold job, especially when I had to work in the sub-zero freezer. The heavy coat they provided was a big help, but after 20 minutes I ran for the exit to warm up. Stocking the cheeses, milk, and dairy cases was more fun and I enjoyed seeing how perfectly I could arrange the displays. It is worthy of note that Leroy was the lord of the schedule and he doled out the much sought after hours according to who produced the best results.

Life at IGA was not all work. On occasion, when I worked in the dairy case, I would suck the gas out of an aerosol whip cream can so I could talk funny to a friend as they walked by, with little regard for the loss Mr. Saunders took on the can that I ruined. It was not unheard of to booby-trap the employee restroom, so a bucket of water would fall on someone on their way out. Stacking huge boxes in front of the cooler door so someone in the cooler couldn't get out was another elementary jokester move. We did manage to have some laughs during the workday.

Nearly a year went by. I had won the approval of Leroy, which earned me my 15 to 20 hours a week on the schedule. In addition, Indiana had passed a landmark minimum wage law that set the wage at $1.00 per hour. I remember Mr. Saunders being irate with the passage and saying that Leroy was the only one who deserved that kind of money, but he reluctantly paid it and moved Leroy's rate up a little higher. Little did Mr. Saunders know he had much bigger problems on the horizon than the new minimum wage. Leroy approached me and told me that if I wanted more hours I could work in the meat department as a clean-up boy. Well, I immediately jumped at the opportunity and reported to Harry, who was a big burly German man with muscular arms and a heavy German accent. One of the meat department clerks met me at five o'clock to explain my clean up duties and my first impression was that it made me a little sick to my stomach. The tables had blood on them and barrels of bones and meat trimmings were sitting around.

When I looked inside of the large walk-in cooler I was greeted with rolls of beef quarter-carcasses that would be cut up, trimmed and turned into steaks, roasts and ground beef to be sold over the counter. I found the whole thing sort of weird and gruesome in a strange way, but I needed the money and listened intently as the clerk explained to me how to clean up the place at night. I tried to put the thought of blood out of my mind and I proceeded to scrape and scrub the large wooden butcher blocks and bleach them down for a fresh clean look for the next morning.

All the large butcher knives and utensils also had to be cleaned along with piles of pans that I washed in a giant sink with plenty of hot soapy water. I would clean from the top down in the meat department, which included walls and cabinets. The last thing was to scrub the floor after a good sweeping of the blood spattered sawdust that covered the floor. Despite my early nausea I managed to get through it and was quite happy when it came time to spread the fresh sawdust over my cleanly scrubbed floor. The sawdust was clean and had a fresh look as it covered the floor evenly. It was actually fun spreading the sawdust so that no footprints showed and it had the appearance of fresh fallen *brown* snow. I evenly coated the entire department without a trace of a footprint and then drew a design or a face in the sawdust. When I finished admiring my masterpiece, I turned off the lights and walked the mile home. I'd take off my soiled shirt and pants and quickly fall to sleep. Thanks a lot Mom for the many times you quietly gathered my clothes and laundered, and even ironed them so they'd be ready to go again…I am sure I must have taken it for granted.

As the weeks progressed Harry seemed satisfied with my work and my sawdust artistry and asked me if I would help with the meat cutting and preparation. At that time, my only experience with knives was making a peanut butter and jelly sandwich at home and I could not comprehend how that skill would serve me.

The knives at work were ten times sharper and quite a bit longer than the ones at home. As I worked side by side with Harry, slowly and cautiously at first, I found out very quickly that knives do cut and it was not long before the sharp blade nicked me. Harry reached for his billfold and gave me a band aid to quickly seal the cut. It's odd how you pick up habits. But from that day until this, I always have a band aid in my own billfold. At first, I found the meat cutting experience sort of weird and I must admit I did not have much of an appetite for meat for a few months. I soon learned to look at the meat cutting as objects that we were transforming into all these perfectly cut and trimmed steaks and chops that were soon to be the beautifully prepared centerpiece of someone's meal. It became a source of pride so I did the job as well as I could. In the short time that I worked in the IGA meat department I basically learned how to hold a knife and do some meat cutting and I learned how to trim the leftover pieces for meat to be used as ground beef. To my amazement one day, Harry went as far as to give me a compliment by saying I was a fast learner but I could stop spending that much time making sure the fresh sawdust was spread just right. Then he gave me a wink and walked away.

CHAPTER 4

SORRY! MR. DeFABIS

Just a half mile down the street from the IGA was a site where a new building was being constructed. By springtime the building was nearly completed a sign went up announcing the impending opening of a new supermarket by the Defabis brothers of Indianapolis.

The store was called Safeway Foods; not to be confused with the giant chain of Safeway stores that operated in other states. Actually the Defabis brothers had used the name before the big chain and had the exclusive on the name in Indiana. They already had a successful store in Indianapolis and thought Brownsburg would be a good place to expand since it was an up and coming community.

When the DeFabis supermarket opened in Brownsburg it was an instant success. Everything was sparkling new and with the latest in supermarket design, it left the aging IGA, with little chance to compete and survive against the Defabis brother's latest and grandest store just down the street. Within months the IGA was finished.

I took a few months off as I was finishing my junior year of high school and playing high school basketball. I didn't have much time to work even part time. However, I did get the bug to work again and decided to see if I could get a job at the Defabis's new store. I introduced myself to the store manager Phil Defabis. He was the older brother and when I told him I had experience in the meat department he sent me back to see his brother Mike in the meat and deli department. They didn't even ask to see my altered birth certificate.

Mike Defabis was a well-dressed, thirty something, your old handsome Italian guy that was full of charisma. He was very well spoken and seemed to take a genuine interest in my desire to work for him. I told him my *experience* with meat cutting and he bought it. Their need for experienced employees to keep pace with the demands of their very busy store probably had a lot to do with getting the job.

I was amazed when I toured the market. There were 60 feet of beautifully polished and buffed stainless steel meat cases, trimmed with oak wood and loaded with an assortment of every kind of beefsteak, chop, ground beef choices and many things I had never even seen at the old IGA, which had just basic cuts that were packaged and displayed in a much simpler manner.

There was perfectly laid oak flooring behind the meat counter that ran the entire length of the meat cases and continued into the large deli department. The deli offered everything from fried and baked chicken to a wide selection of cold cuts, salami and cheese to fresh salads and even fresh made pies.

Large rolls of white wrapping paper were anchored to the back of the display cases at six foot intervals above the oak wrapping counters behind the cases. The store was way ahead of its time for the Indianapolis area; and I was awestricken by the uniqueness and beauty of it all.

I was introduced to Ed, an older gentleman, who was the meat department manager. He was a wonderful, kind, but no nonsense kind of guy, who I later found out had fought in several major battles of WWII and suffered a severe hearing loss as a result. John, another journeyman meat cutter in his thirties was a jolly guy who was quick to laugh and obviously loved to eat judging by the size of his girth. Max was also in his thirties and was an intense chain smoker who was always in a hurry. They were the guys, along with Mike Defabis, with whom I was assigned to work. Little did I know they would have such a major impact on my life's work.

I was perfecting the skills needed to become a journeyman meat cutter. We went from item to item in the long meat cases replenishing the items that were running low. There was a learning curve required to develop the skill needed to cut and prepare each product. It took extra sharp knives and endless practice to make the cuts and trims just right to avoid the disappointing stare from Brother Mike when a cut was incorrect or the display was a little messy. Mike demanded perfection and I quickly learned to do the job correctly. His demand for perfection was the reason for his success. Unfortunately, my youth and inexperience led to numerous screw-ups and a constant target of one of Mike's *looks*.

The most memorable occasion was one Saturday morning when, as an apprentice, I was assigned the job of grinding several hundred pounds of hamburger in a giant grinding machine. The hamburger was on special and people were buying it as fast as I could make it.

The machine had a large chrome chute into which the meat was dropped. It would then pass through a blade that cut the meat and forced it through a round metal plate where the beef was actually ground and would emerge in the familiar spaghetti shape. My job was to push the meat through the metal tube to produce the ground beef. Every fifteen minutes or so I would stop the machine and change the size of the plate and clean the cutting knives. Well, with my youthful inexperience and rush to keep up with the demand, I inadvertently left one of the changed cutting blades in the hopper of meat waiting to be ground.

When the machine was restarted, there was a loud clank, followed by smoke and the realization that I had locked up the entire grinding machine…I knew I was in big trouble. The timing was perfect; it was a busy Saturday; hamburger was on special and there was a crowd of customers who could not seem to buy enough. My face was bright red and my heart was pounding as Mike came running over to see what the hell apprentice Randy had screwed this time. Putting it mildly, it was quite unpleasant. Mike was standing there screaming, "If it is what I fuckin' think it is your fuckin' ass is fired!"

I sheepishly stood there as he disassembled the machine to discover it was *exactly* what he *fuckin'* thought it was and I knew my *fuckin'* ass was in a lot of trouble. The grinder was totally locked up and ruined. Obviously the machine was designed to grind meat…*not metal!*

Well, not only was smoke pouring from the machine but also from Mike's eyes as he launched into what seemed like a forever rage. He called his brother at the store 40 miles away and they spent the rest of the day shuttling fresh ground beef to Brownsburg from Indianapolis to satisfy the terrific demand of our customers. I kept my head down and never spoke another word the whole day. When things calmed down and we made it through the day, I learned to my surprise that I still had my job and was allowed to operate the new grinder that arrived Monday morning. I did learn an important lesson, though…always know where the extra metal cutting blades were before turning on the machine.

Afterward, big John kidded me endlessly about my hamburger making skills. His great sense of humor and happy demeanor, made working with Big John a lot of fun. He was from a very strict Baptist family and not only loved to eat but was obsessed with Indiana's favorite past time…basketball. He was married and free of the constraints of his strict conservative religious upbringing, so he bet regularly on the outcome of all the basketball games. He was quite good at it and he seemed to have an uncanny ability to pick winners. Being right more than wrong; he made a lot of extra cash with his pastime. He was quite generous with his winnings and we would often jump into his old Nash and head to Steve's Stew House or a buffet in Indianapolis to enjoy his other favorite pastime…eating!

As the months working with the DeFabis family slid by, I was making fewer mistakes and getting into trouble less often. There were still many occasions when I made miscues on expensive cuts of meat, but John or Max would cover for me by correcting the trim or by grinding the miss-cuts into ground beef as a last resort. Learning the trade took time. Not only did I have to develop knife cutting skills, but I had to keep the knives razor sharp. Dull knives did not cut smoothly and were dangerous… sharp knives made quick, clean and smooth cuts.

Learning the art of meat cutting made it imperative to know not only how to sharpen a knife correctly, but also to understand the intricacies of holding the knife and applying the correct pressure for each cut. That could only be learned with experience. I was working side by side with the skilled meat cutters and most often doing the lesser skilled assistance type jobs. But it gave me the opportunity to observe the journeyman's skills until I had the opportunities to apply what I was learning.

The market regularly received mammoth quarters of prime beef that weighed approximately 200 pounds. We had to hang them on rolling hooks so they could be moved to the preparation room where they were carved into the beautiful steaks, roasts and chops to be displayed in our grand showcase.

Journeyman meat cutters made the cuts in precisely the right places to effect the correct separations between more expensive steaks and the sections that might be used for less expensive roasts or ground beef. The market's profit hinged on those cuts being consistently perfect. It was uncanny how the journeyman meat cutters knew exactly where to make the cut and did so automatically by identifying different muscles or characteristics on the quarter of beef they we're butchering.

Those meat cutting procedures were performed at a rapid pace because of the endless list of other tasks with constant deadlines. Consequently, they would not allow me to touch one of those pieces without one of the experienced guys standing there to guide me through it. I look back and appreciate the patience they had for my lack of skill.

The payback for my inexperience was assignments to less skilled jobs in addition to assisting the journeyman by anticipating their next move and having the tools and utensils ready for the procedure...almost like assisting a surgeon in the operating room. After I had been working with different meat cuts for a while, I reached a point where I could identify from the muscle structures, texture, color and grain exactly from which part of the carcass it had been cut. By making the association of the meat cuts to parts of the carcass, I thought less about the fact we were cutting up animals.

Most meat markets had a large electric table saw that was used to save time cutting through bones. The table saw stood eight feet tall and had a super sharp blade that spun around at a buzz saw speed and zipped right through the bones instantly. Unfortunately it could zip through a human's finger with the same efficiency. When I worked on the saw, I did so with all of my attention focused on the job to avoid becoming a casualty. Since there were no safety mechanisms in use, I was acutely aware of the location of my hands at all times.

One of the things the Defabis boys took pride in was the fact all chickens were cut by hand. Learning to cut a chicken involved knowing where the joints were and making the cuts. The pieces were neatly placed in a cardboard container for display. The whole process took about three minutes per chicken once I was up to speed. That method was fine until there was a special on chickens and we sold twenty times the normal amount. The only way to keep up was to cut the chickens on the table saw. One guy would run the saw and make the cuts while another would catch the pieces as they passed through the saw and package them. I was the catcher at first and then I had the chance to be the saw operator. I couldn't believe they would trust me. The chicken had to be passed through the blade at the proper angle to achieve the correct cut. The whole process was a team effort and to my surprise, I actually became quite adept at it.

I quickly learned to make the proper cuts and could cut the chicken up in 5 or 6 seconds with the help of the power saw. Being young and with little or no fear, I would cut hundreds of chickens at a steady pace for hours with my fingers only an inch from the blade…I became the fastest by far.

Being older and wiser, I look back and realize how dangerous and crazy that was. The journeymen were probably too smart to work at that speed so close to an unforgiving danger. But the job did get done and I looked at it, in my demented way, as carrying my load with the older guys and it was a source of pride. I shudder at the thought of how easy it would have been to lose a finger or hand.

Today the process of meat cutting at the supermarket level has been streamlined and the larger quarters of beef are cut down into much smaller pieces before they are shipped to the stores to make the final cuts. Today's meat cutters have no clue as to how to break down the 200 pound quarters.

I didn't realize it at the time, but the experience working with the Defabis brothers at Safeway and the business principles to which I was exposed became the foundation I would build upon when I struck out on my own, as it turned out, in just a few years.

The Defabis brothers ran a super clean, modern, and well stocked store that was staffed with carefully selected friendly workers. They were taught the true meaning of the concept of the customer always being right and how to go about pleasing them. That principle was carried out to the extreme. The leader of it all was Mike Defabis; a guy with movie star good looks who was always friendly to the customer and acknowledged everyone with whom he came in contact. He dressed impeccably with crisp ironed clothes, shiny shoes and perfectly groomed hair. There was no doubt about who was the leader. He portrayed such an air of success people couldn't help but want to please him and jump on the bandwagon. At that age, I admired Mike and was happy when I would earn his approval for my job performance. That was when I was not destroying expensive meat grinding machines.

When I looked at other markets, I noticed how the unusual things we did at Safeway, made us a more interesting place to shop. Not only did we display unique cuts of meat, but we offered different items from freshly prepared Salisbury steaks and ready to bake meat items ham loafs and specially seasoned chopped steaks...plus everything was top quality. I took it upon myself to make sure all the best items were on display, with a sign, and always freshly stocked. I could tell Mike was pleased that I did this on my own.

Mike had a special sign making kit where he would sit and make small 3x5 signs that would describe items throughout the store. These little *shelf talkers* praised the item in just a few short words and displayed the price. They were quickly and colorfully made with Mike's beautiful touch for precise lettering and color combinations. I stood and watched him while I was on break and at night when he wasn't around I practiced my strokes and the wording of the message. He had a flare for it which made them look classy. I was fascinated and realized the importance of the message subtly delivered by those cards...it was my first exposure to Marketing 101.

Mike Defabis was a busy man. He was usually like a whirlwind, running between the three stores they owned. Since he was not around our store as much, I took it upon myself to start creating the shelf *talker signs*. Being left-handed I often found myself smearing the ink if I were not careful with the way I made the sign. I usually found myself printing the sign from right to left to avoid smearing the ink and ruining my little creation.

With practice I got rather clever with the system and it became quite natural to technically create the sign backwards. I was developing a vocabulary for words that were sellers or eye grabbers...

Special Today• Made from •Scratch• Just Arrived• New• Try it• Freshly Made• Today's Feature•

Like Mike's signs the sell had to be subtle and in just a few words.

Soon my signs made their big debut and I would ask the store department managers about an item that was new or unusual or something they wanted to push. I loved the layout and color blending that would create a sign combining all the elements of a *perfect sell*, and I was proud that the sign would be completed in a flurry of quick strokes and rapid fire thought. The biggest stamp of approval came when Mike approached me and said he wanted to talk to me about these signs that were popping up all over the store. Of course, I braced myself for a barrage of negative reviews, but Mike paused for a second and said my signs were as good as the ones he made and to keep up the good work. My first foray into advertising was a success and just another skill that I could possibly use in the future.

CHAPTER 5

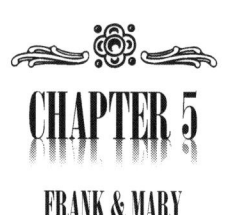

FRANK & MARY

I enjoyed going to work at the supermarket and relished the camaraderie and day to day interaction with the boys. When we got overstocked with chicken wings, Big John seasoned 30 or 40 of them and threw them into the pressure fryer …eight minutes later we would have a feast of fried morsels. We still made our extended lunch hour runs into Indianapolis to search out a dive that served a killer bowl of chili or stew. We made frequent trips to cafeteria style restaurants; which at that time had a real flair for true home style cooking and flavor. We traveled to little Indiana burgs in search of some food specialty to pig out on.

Whether it was a restaurant that served home cooked food or someone who served fresh mushrooms, Big John would travel the state looking for hole-in-the-wall catfish specialty restaurants or maybe the perfect fried chicken. A favorite treat in Indiana and the Midwest is the pork tenderloin sandwich. The tenderloin was a thick boneless pork chop that would be pounded out with a mallet or cleaver until it was a paper thin and about the size of a saucer. It was then spiced and dipped in egg and a mixture of breadcrumbs or flour and cornmeal and sautéed in oil or French fried to a golden brown in just a few minutes. The creation was then served on a ridiculously large fresh round bun with the tenderloin dwarfing the bun. Lettuce, tomato, Hellmann's mayonnaise and a scoop of fresh fries and you were in for a real taste treat.

In Indiana, a restaurant's success hinged on the ability to create the perfect pork tenderloin sandwich. Coffee shops and cafes prided themselves on their version of the sandwich. None was better than Frank and Mary's Tavern on Main Street in Brownsburg. Frank ran the long wooden bar on one side of the tavern, while his wife was stationed in a cubby hole of a kitchen on the other side to the rear of the room. It wasn't fancy by any stretch of the imagination and the beat up wood floors and beer advertising on the walls gave it a certain feel.

I don't know if a Hollywood set designer could have created a better 40ish looking joint. But on a cold, windy Indiana day and a hunger in your belly it felt good to swing the door open and smell the aroma of Mary's tenderloin's percolating in the giant iron skillets. You knew in just a short time, after first bite, all would be well again. At Frank and Mary's it just wasn't about the food, it included entertainment.

Frank was pale from having spent so much time indoors behind a bar during the day. He was a skinny guy with faded tattoos and a gruff manner of speech. He took great delight in sliding beer bottles from one end of the bar to the other and tossing empties ten or fifteen feet across the back of the counter into the trash can. I don't ever recall one breaking or a sliding beer bottle flipping over. All the while Frank would be voicing his opinion about Indiana basketball, politics or perhaps the bitter cold and his constant yearning for a vacation.

His wife, Mary contributed equally to the essence of the place. She was manning the kitchen by herself and shouting at a couple of waitresses to get the damn food to this table or that one. Pork tenderloins were flying out of there as fast as Mary could make them. The sandwiches were huge and were garnished with French fries or Mary's unbelievable potato salad and a cup of her to die for homemade coleslaw.

The highlight of a visit would be the banter between Frank and Mary during the organized chaos in the heat of the constant rush. He yelled at her about the time it was taking for an order, "What the hell's going on back there; the customers are starving!" She yelled back, "I'm only one person and if you don't like it, stick it where the sun don't shine."

Everyone got a big laugh at Frank's exaggerations and Mary's perfect come backs. It was all good natured. Occasionally there was a wink from Frank or a perky smile crossed Mary's' face when she delivered the good natured punch line. Late in the lunch rush, it wasn't unusual for the kitchen to finally run out of the tenderloin sandwich. That served as an added incentive to make an early lunch run to Frank and Mary's Tavern.

As a teenager, I often drove down County Line Road in my old 56 Chevy. A few miles out of Clermont, there was a spectacular rambling brick ranch style home that could not be missed. It was actually like an estate. I always wondered who lived there and how anyone could afford a house like that.

While working at the Defabis brothers market as a meat cutter in training I was approached by a high school friend, Steve Hoagland. He asked if I could do his dad a favor and help watch his meat counter for a day because his regular butcher was off. Always looking to pick up a little extra money I readily agreed. I vaguely remembered that the family owned a little country store in Clermont, the next town over from Brownsburg.

That Saturday morning I pulled up to Hoagies Clermont Market and General Store. I had no idea what to expect. A fair sized wood frame building sat on the corner. The front porch which spanned the entire length of the building was loaded with plants, garden supplies, buckets, even rocking chairs. I squeezed my way past the merchandise on the porch to the front door. My senses were overcome by a place that was stuffed to the brim with grocery items, dry goods, household items, brooms, and shovels...the works. Baskets piled high with fresh vegetables lined the main aisle back to the meat counter and deli section. The wonderful aroma of the fruits, spices and cooked meats wafted in the air where it blended with the smells of the merchandise hanging from the ceiling. It was like walking into the main tent at the circus and not knowing what to look at first.

While I was attempting to absorb the sights and smells, I was greeted by Hoagie, the ringmaster himself. He was just an average sized man...not real tall...not real short...in his fifties. His recently dyed jet black hair was arranged in a perfect comb-over, if there is such a thing. He was wearing a freshly pressed white shirt and apron.

"Hello I'm Hoagie," he said with a smile that lit up his entire face. He was very sincere and gracious thanking me for my willingness to help him that day. He showed me around and explained where everything was that I would require for my job. Hoagie was truly the star of the show…he called everyone by name as he hustled around the store filling orders, pointing out specials and all the while asking customers about their kids and what was going on in their lives. Of course, there was always the occasional joke. It was apparent that he was glad to see them and wanted to please.

When the day began to wind down, I was grateful when we sat down for a breather on the old front porch. By then, I was truly in awe of Hoagie's high energy and the efficiency of the entire operation.

I asked him several questions about running the business and who ran the store when he got sick. He replied, "Randy when you have a business you are not permitted to ever get sick." I was in awe. As it turned out, that the rambling brick estate on County Line Road was Hoagies house. I didn't quite understand how his family always disappeared for a few weeks in the dead of winter for a Florida vacation at the Fontainebleau Hotel in Miami Beach. His two kids had his same wonderful temperament and disposition and wore nothing but the best clothes.

There was never a dull moment working alongside the characters at Safeway, but I really didn't know what I wanted to do with my life. I took a few courses at the Indiana University extension school in Indianapolis and achieved decent grades, but I felt the nagging need to try something different.

CHAPTER 6

FACTORY LIFE

My friend Montie had landed a coveted job fifteen miles down the road in Speedway, Indiana at Linde Aire Company, a division of Union Carbide. He offered to put in a good word for me if I were interested. At the time factory work was a secure job and the prospect of working there appealed to me.

The plant was like a mini-city of brick, multi-storied buildings situated on 50 or 60 acres of prime property, directly across the street from the Indianapolis 500 race track. The centerpiece was a five or six story smoke stack jutting into the air which announced in giant vertical letters painted on the stack, **LINDE AIRE**. The tall paned windows of the buildings had years of accumulated smoke and grime which, in an odd way, lent character to the factory.

I stumbled into the employment office and was escorted through a maze of offices. I landed at the desk of a suit and tie guy named Ron Dick. He explained that The Company not only produced liquid gases, but also made *Eveready* flashlight batteries, welding tanks and cubic zirconia gems. Linde Aire also had a government contract to make the pipe that carried the liquid nitrogen to the space shuttle at Cape Canaveral. In deference to Montie, he told me I could start on Monday and was issued a yellow plastic I.D. badge. My employee number was 2406. That number was very important because everything in the factory was based on seniority. If a new job was posted the employee with the lowest number got the job.

My new brother-in-law, Richard (Red) Kramer got a job at the factory a few days after I was hired. Naturally, he had a higher employee number and I always teased him that I could outbid him for a job because of my lower number. Richard was a 6'4" tall, red-headed, basketball star at Tech High School in Indianapolis. He had been offered several college scholarships, among them a full scholarship at Corpus Christi University in Texas, which he had declined. After a year of factory life, he realized that there was no future and contacted the university to see if the scholarship were still available. Fortunately for him, even though it had been three years since he had been offered the scholarship, it was. He moved with my sister and their two children to Texas where he had a very successful basketball career, got a great education and went on to a successful career in finance.

My first day inside the huge brick building was an awesome experience. I was equipped with a lunch bucket and safety glasses and was ready to go.

The building housed hundreds of machines like lathes, drills and sanders. I was hired to be a machine operator, but I didn't think I could ever learn to operate all those machines

Subsequently, the supervisor sat me down at a giant drill press and showed me how to drill holes in brass-fittings at a preset position exactly as specified in the blueprint. There were guides and stops so it was nearly impossible to screw up the piece. The ever present quality control guy would measure the pieces randomly to make sure everything was up to spec. After about an hour, I finished drilling the fittings in the first box, so they brought me a stack of boxes with enough blank fittings to last for several days. The occasional need to change a drill bit was the only break in the monotony.

The day was controlled by bells. At break time, a bell rang signaling me to go to a roped off area to hang out for ten minutes. At lunch time, the same bell rang to direct me back to the same roped off area, this time for 30 minutes to enjoy the always delicious boxed lunch I prepared at 6:00 that morning with no incentive or effort to be creative or healthy, to be enjoyed in the dark grey confines of a factory

Once the day ended and the bell sounded everyone would proceed to the time clock line to punch out at the precise moment the little hand rested on the 4 and the big hand landed on the 12. Then the mad race began; past the guardhouse, through the chain link fence, and to the parking lot to jump in the cars for their getaway. Like the Grand Prix in Monaco, the object was to be the first one through the gate.

I was surprised to find out after a few short weeks, that I had learned to operate almost every one of those machines that scared me the first day. If the truth be told, they required little skill, as they were preset to eliminate mistakes. I tried other work stations in the factory and learned the ins and outs of how a factory operated.

There was a time study guy with a clip board and stop watch who followed everybody around to study each and every motion to achieve maximum production. When my turn came to be studied, I was approached by an older and wiser union worker warning me to slow down and make every move slowly and precisely so the time study would not reflect that the work could be done faster. Being a young ambitious, 19-year-old I found it painstaking and somewhat silly to move in slow motion. But I did my best and when the results came back the older union guys were a little pissed at me, to say the least, as the rates were altered to my faster pace. One thing I did get out of the time study was how to break down every task into the position of the hands and the motion needed to perform the desired result.

I found it amazing, and quite frankly, ridiculous that a job was created just to study the task of movement. I couldn't help but wonder what a boring career it must be to click a stop-watch all day, every day, year after year. It wasn't just the time study guy, but there were a countless number of mundane and boring jobs at the factory. Once, I asked a fellow employee walking by to help me lift a box of brass fittings to a position next to where I was working. He said, "Oh no…you have to call an equipment mover to help you; that's not my classification." I waited twenty minutes for an equipment mover to arrive to lift the box 36 inches.

The mentality of the workers was to take it nice and easy to make the task last all day if possible. To make sure the workers stayed with the program there were the union stewards who watched over the flock to insure the company was not taking advantage of the workers. It was definitely a *them* against *us* attitude. If anyone got out of line, the *boys* would, have *a little talk* to remind them whose side they were on.

I went along with the program and fell in line; after all, I was making three times what I earned as a meat cutter in training and there were benefits; paid sick days, paid holidays, overtime pay, and insurance. To make it even better, the factory had a nice juicy government contract for the space program and I could work all the overtime hours I wanted. I jumped all over that and found myself working seven days a week with plenty of incentives to work more.

I switched job stations around the factory as much as possible to break up the ever present repetitious monotony of doing the same thing over and over. One week I assisted a painter, the next I took the all-important job of equipment mover. I even did a stretch as on oven tender which required that I sit in a behemoth full of ovens. Each was the size of a garage full of cylinders being heated at 550 degrees. For what purpose? Hell, I had no clue, but I did little else than sit in a chair looking at temperature gauges and doing very little else...it seemed like pretty easy money. A couple times during the shift, when the time was up, I had to go into the oven and remove the cylinders. The fastest I ever moved in my life was when I went into a 550 degree oven to grab the cylinders and get the hell out. Time study or no time study, union guy or no union guy; I was hell bent on setting the world speed record for moving cylinders out of a 550 degree oven!

One benefit of watching oven gauges happened when lunch time rolled around. I had the bright idea of bringing a TV dinner to place in the giant oven. I ate like a king on Swanson Hungry Man meatloaf dinners.

Time would drag on so slowly with nothing to do, I eventually became bored with the oven-tender job and got an assignment as a pipe cleaner in the section of the factory that was preparing the pipes used for fueling the shuttles to be shipped to Florida. What a crock that job was. It required tying a ball of rags on the end of a cable, squirting the rags with alcohol and running around to the other end of 50 foot, 8 inch round pipe, where I then proceed to pull the rags through the pipe to clean the interior. I repeated that over and over while the inspector watched until the ball of rags emerged clean. It took two of us working very slowly to accomplish the task to the delight of George, our union steward

The inspections were even more bazaar; they consisted of pulling a clean ball of rags through the pipe to see if they made their way through free of dirt. We learned that to pass the inspection, was simply a matter of not making the ball of rags too snug, so they would not touch but twenty percent of the interior surface. The inspector really was not overly concerned…he was just interested in getting to the end of the shift. After an eight hour shift, they would ask if I'd work overtime for double pay. It was typical to work sixteen hour days or even more if I could handle the boredom.

After weeks of this I would have given anything for a day off. I finally passed up quadruple pay just to keep my sanity. There was a lot of comic relief working the crazy long hours with often times really weird people. There was a guy named Wilbur from Kentucky. He had a wild look in his eyes and was…how can I put this…quite *dentally* challenged. I couldn't begin to comprehend what his home life was like with eight kids at home. It was easy to understand why he worked whatever hours they threw at him.

Wilber was no dummy when it came to feeding his family. There was very little supervision at night as I toiled away at my pipe cleaning job. As a matter of fact, people were taking turns sleeping in the nurse's office. Wilbur had the bright idea of making makeshift traps for rabbits. The factory grounds were huge and had several open field areas. Rabbits were quite a delicacy in Indiana. He would religiously set his traps when he came to work. Later that the night he would go check his traps and more times than not he would score.

Wilbur would proceed to skin and dress his catch in true Daniel Boone Kentucky tradition. The clever part of the process, and to prove that Wilbur was truly a genius; he took his catch to the liquid nitrogen section of the factory and dipped each perfectly cleaned rabbit into the tank of liquid nitrogen. To my amazement the rabbits froze instantly. I confirmed the process when I removed an orange from my lunch box and dipped it into the nitrogen; seconds later I was holding a big orange rock. All I could say was, *"Damnnn Wilber!"* Wilbur would then tuck his prized catch into his empty lunch box at the end of his shift and head home.

A year into my factory career, *it seemed like five*, I was still making all the overtime I could mentally handle. But I had serious doubts about factory work being my life's calling. Sure the money was good, but each day of work was drudgery. I began to look around at the old guys who had spent their lives in this tedious, repetitious workplace moving to the bells and whistles of the factory and would often see empty robots staring back at me. Ed, the factory painter, always told me to find another career. He turned out to be quite prophetic when he told me the industrialized days in our country were limited; the unions had overstepped their boundaries and big changes were coming. As Ed foresaw, there were big changes to factory work and it was not too many years thereafter, that the factory was closed.

I could not see myself doing this for thirty years and becoming swallowed into the robotic existence. Besides, I wasn't real confident that the space shuttle pipes I had cleaned would work on the first flight. I had visions of the whole damn thing blowing up and federal agents looking for the young factory worker back in Indiana who did a half-assed job cleaning the pipes and cost the country millions of dollars. I concluded that if you didn't enjoy your work a large chunk of your life would be miserable. I'm sure a lot of young men reached this *come to Jesus moment,* but it sure scared the hell out of me. I thought about how much I enjoyed working for the Defabis brothers in the meat department and how I liked going to work. At least the time flew and there was not so much drudgery. Despite most everyone around me saying I was nuts for quitting the factory and all the high pay, I went back to Safeway and asked for my old job back at less than half the pay.

Mike Defabis had no hesitation taking me back. He must have forgotten about the meat grinder incident. I made the proverbial confession that I was not happy with factory life and would give my all to the Safeway cause.

Mike either believed me or he was desperate for help. I would like to have thought that he missed my sign making skills. I was making the signs again in less than a week. Life and work was once again fun. John, Max, Lloyd and the others were enjoying our chicken wing feast once more. John was funnier than ever and I was even learning more about meat cutting and the deli section of the business. Along with what I perceived as a lot of valuable knowledge, I was honing my skills and overcoming my shyness by waiting on customers and selling them the different cuts of meat. Mike was a real pro. I listened as he worked the counter and so effortlessly sold the different cuts and quickly wrapped the order. I learned from him and realized that salesmanship was indeed an art, and I intended to master it.

One person working the counter was an elderly gentleman named Bob Lawson. Bob had owned a little country store in Danville, Indiana. As times changed a supermarket came into the small town and Bob was forced out of business. Bob would make the hour drive over to Brownsburg and work the meat counter. I'm sure he was delighted to have the opportunity, although, he of acted like we were lucky to have him. To show that he really didn't need the money he would open his wallet when the checks were passed out to reveal a stack of past checks he had never bothered to cash.

When Bob arrived for work it was a ritual. He not only arrived an hour early but had a whole routine. He was clean shaven with a generous splash of Old Spice after shave applied. Naturally, he was perfectly dressed in a flawlessly starched white shirt and a fresh white hat that he placed on his head with precision. His marking pencils were all fully checked and loaded with the thick black crayons. His nails were scrubbed and manicured. The fresh white linen apron was put on with the care and exactness of a matador preparing for a bullfight. He carried himself with total confidence behind the counter and looked like he owned the joint.

I remembered the first day he started, he came from a little corner grocery store and knew very little about meat; and even less about all the different choices we offered in our huge display. I had to spend a lot of time showing him the cuts and constantly helping him answer customer requests. But old Bob was the wizard and he had the gift of gab. Within days he ditched me and took over.

It was no time before he had the customer eating out of his hand. If Bob gave a selection his seal of approval then it was sold. Housewives would wait for Bob to wait on them and if he wasn't available Mike would come by with his good looks and charm them to finish a sale. I was so young and wet behind the ears that when I waited on the customers there were occasions when Bob would have to give his approval to the chops or roast that I had selected, even though he didn't know the names of the cuts just a few months earlier. I wondered if I would ever look old enough for customers to accept my word as the *Holy Grail*? Oh well, there were valuable lessons to be learned about confidence and salesmanship by watching and listening to Bob and Mike. It really stuck with me as I moved forward.

Another year at Safeway and at twenty years old, I felt pressure to be doing something with myself other than work in a grocery store. It was constantly on my mind. I now was married and not only had a wife, but my first daughter, Dawn. I did receive pay raises but would that be enough to support a family? Indiana was termed a right to work state and wage scales were not very high. Deep down inside I realized where my future was heading.

CHAPTER 7

GO WEST YOUNG MAN

Indiana winters seemed to never end. As March rolled around and I was grappling with how to pay my last winter heating bills, I was still searching for the perfect career. Charlie Hilton, my childhood friend, had moved to California when he was fourteen. When I talked to him on his visits back to Indiana he painted such a pretty picture of life in California …warm days and the beaches. Charlie worked in California as a supermarket manager and told me how good the pay was in unionized supermarkets; especially for meat cutters. It did not take much convincing for me to give California a shot after going through an unusually cold Indiana winter and faced with a heat bill that seemed like the national debt.

Within days, I broke the news to everyone and was making my escape plan. My dad loaned me his big yellow Chrysler Newport; we hooked up a rental trailer loaded with our few belongings and took off. As the Beach Boys lyrics said, "Going out west where I belong." Since I seldom ventured out of Indiana, I was amazed when I got to Oklahoma and looked out over the wide open spaces. It took me four days to finally come out of the Cajon Pass and into the valley in San Bernardino, California. Never being around mountains, I couldn't believe the beauty of it all. Luckily it was a smog free day. The vast population flabbergasted me; and one city hooked to another for miles and miles. I was staying at my wife's grandmother's two-story, early California home in Lincoln Park, in the city of Pomona, which was lined with big trees and those swaying palms everywhere. I don't recall swaying palms in Indiana. California was something else. I was too young and amazed to let reality set in.

The first non-family person I met was the next door neighbor, who was a strong, muscular brute of a guy employed as a roofer. He was the ultimate do-it-your-selfer. His house was constantly under construction. He went so far as to have a rented bulldozer parked in the front yard. His name was Mike Egan. He was a true character and it was a fortunate day when I met him.

The very next morning I received directions to El Montie, California from Mike, who couldn't do enough to help. The only problem was he was an Irish emigrant and I couldn't understand a word he said. But I smiled and took his advice and maps. So I set out in my dad's big old Chrysler to search for a job. It was my first time driving on a freeway before. I was a little freaked out as I headed down the San Bernardino freeway toward Los Angeles…but I was on a big adventure.

I couldn't believe there were five lanes of traffic and cars were whizzing by me like I was standing still. I had to adapt rather quickly if I were going to be a Californian. I did manage to get off the freeway without getting killed or creating a *road rage* incident and found Lower Azusa Canyon Rd., where the offices of Vons Supermarkets were located. After filling out an application and getting to do an interview, I was in for my first big surprise in the Golden State. *They hired me!*

I was trying to show as much confidence as I could muster during the interview and I stretched the truth when I said I was a journeyman meat cutter, but by some stroke of luck I was hired and even more amazing, I was to report to work the next day to store number 86 in Hacienda Heights, California…wherever the hell that was!

I made the long drive back to Pomona and I remembered the astonishment on grandma's face when I told her I was starting work the next day. "Oh…and where is Hacienda Heights?" I stumbled next door to where the friendly Irishman lived and asked directions to Hacienda Heights. Mike, just like before, took out some maps and explained in his Irish accent how to get there. I still couldn't understand a word he was saying.

I did know how to read a map, so the next morning I woke up very early and wheeled the big starship out of the narrow driveway and was off to work. It took over an hour to get there and I felt very lucky to find it after stopping and asking a few people. Hacienda Heights was an upscale suburb of Los Angeles.

I reported to the manager of the meat department, Ross

Prather and took a look around at the long meat display stretched out in front of me. There were cuts, shapes and items on display that I could not identify. California meat cutting was a lot more sophisticated than back home. I came to realize very quickly that I was in over my head. I got a break when Ross put me to work side by side with a tall, skinny guy named Jim Jones from Arkansas. It didn't take Jim long to figure out that by West Coast standards I unqualified as a journeyman. He saw that the skill level I brought with me from Indiana didn't compare to a true journeyman's union standards. Jim, and I knew I had a whole lot to learn. If I wanted to be a meat cutter in California, I had better learn it fast.

This particular Vons was an extremely high volume store, ranked among the top in the chain. They employed six journeyman meat cutters and all were top notch. The pace of work was much faster than I had encountered back in little Brownsburg, Indiana. Lucky for me, Jimmie Jones had me work with him so he could hide my lack of knowledge and give me a crash course in California style meat cutting. He would position me in the 32 degree cooler and let me grind hamburger, a less skilled job and one that I did know from my Indiana days. All the guys I worked with were from other states and had migrated to California. I began to realize that nobody in California was a native Californian. Howie was from Oklahoma and Ross was from Oregon and there was a new guy that had just started from a place called Long Island, New York.

His name was Ben...Ben D'Aquila. Little did I know that Benny was going to play a big role in my life in California. Ben was a few years older than I. He was a handsome and charming Italian man with a wife and four kids. He drove a big Olds station wagon. Unlike me, he had extensive meat cutting experience, in no small part because of his exposure to the many ethnic demands of the diverse population of New York.

He had razor sharp knives and knew how to use them. All of his cuts were executed swiftly and with ease. I think he realized I was a rank amateur and maybe felt a little sorry for me. He also helped me overcome my lack of skills with helpful suggestions and instruction until I was able to bring my skill level up to par.

We hit it off and learned that we didn't live too far from each other. On payday and I looked at my check I couldn't believe my eyes. It was more than double what I earned in Indiana. Ross had been kind to me and gave me journeyman wages even though I had lacked the skills expected in California. I was a member of the Meat Cutters of North American union and received top insurance benefits. Life was good!

With time, I became more in tune with the California style of meat cutting, thanks to Ben and Jimmie and a lot of patience from everyone. What I lacked in knowledge I tried to make for up by staying alert and working hard. I began to understand the business model and budget goals in California. There was an awareness that profit resulted from constant vigilance of the percentage of wage and food cost and productivity. I began to take pride in working in that environment. Every employee had to be sharp and there was zero tolerance for anyone who could not perform. It was a good experience.

CHAPTER 8

PARTNERS

Ben and I were taking during a break one morning and he shared his dream of always wanting a business. I too shared this same desire ever since I had seen my childhood friend's family run Hilton's corner market. Ben told me he had found a location that was a small meat market. It was currently closed but he thought he could work a deal with the landlord to get a lease. He hesitated to ask me to be in the venture because he had already asked his brother, Danny, to join him. I could understand; it was a family thing. A few days passed and Ben approached me to say his brother had changed his mind about going into business with him. Seems he worked at Los Angeles Power Company and did not want to give up his benefits and job security.

As I look back, he was a pretty smart, logical guy. But as I came to find out, in my career, a lot of business decisions were not always made on what was logical and smart. And after Bennie asked me to be his partner in the meat shop venture, that was my first and biggest step in forgetting what was logical and only going with what was in my heart. I said, "Yes" ignoring the fact that I had a young family at home and no guarantee of a paycheck in the future. But I did know that I had a burning desire to be an entrepreneur and was full of confidence to go all in to make it succeed. I wholly believed that a lot of entrepreneurs made that first step, dismissed logic and reality and just went for it

If I had a formal four year college education and were a little older, I doubt I would have done it. I looked at it as a now or never choice. I was only 22 years old and thought if things didn't work out I could always go back to being a meat cutter. I readily admit that a lot of my confidence was actually border line ignorance.

Ben also told me I would have to come up with some money for the partnership. I needed a whopping $1000.00 dollars to start it off, but that was only nine hundred ninety-nine dollars more than I had! I was young, married and a recent California transplant I was by all methods of basic accounting…broke. But measured against to missing my opportunity of a lifetime…what should I do?

After pondering my few choices, *do it or don't do it*, I knew I had to get on the phone and call the only banker I knew…my dad. It took me a day to get my nerve up to make that fateful call. I took my afternoon break and walked to the phone booth in front of the Vons Market on Hacienda Ave. My knees were shaking as I dialed the phone number back in Indiana.

My father was a man of few words. He was a man's man who worked his whole life on the New York Central Railroad as a switchman. He was raised on a farm in Illinois and knew what it was to work hard and spend every penny wisely. He went to church on Sundays, lived by a strict moral code, a strong code of ethics and expected the same from his kids. If anyone crossed him, he didn't hesitate to straighten them out. I watched my older brother Sonny try to buck him once and I saw the results. That's why I always kept a low profile around him and made sure I didn't do anything to get him too upset with me.

My oldest sister, Jackie was always the clever one in the family and always figured out how to get around Dad

Money was never discussed and I didn't remember too many times I ever asked him for a dime. On the rare occasion he decided to give us a dollar, he always checked twice to make sure two weren't stuck together. I look back and certainly don't fault him for his frugal ways with money.

In all fairness, we truly never wanted for anything and it was a lesson that the "best things in life are free". Material things were not at the top of the list but all of what's truly important in life was magically being instilled in us. I adored my dad.

I stood in a phone booth 2300 miles away getting ready to ask my dad for a thousand dollars for me to gamble on a hair brained business venture. When I heard his voice on the phone, I just about lost my nerve, but after stammering through some small talk I blurted out the reason for my call. To my utter surprise, after a brief pause, he agreed to loan me the money.

When I told my boss at Vons we were leaving to go into business he asked twice if I was sure I wanted to do this. Ross was a lot older than I and he knew I was taking a very risky step with little chance to make it. I gulped and said "Yes".

Monday morning Ben and I jumped in the car to drive the hour from Pomona California to Downey to start building our fortune. I had not seen the place and just took Ben's word for it. That was not a real smart way to succeed in business, but that was my big opportunity and there was no room for common sense or sound business decisions!

We drove all over Downey looking for Meralta Square Shopping Center. We found it on the main street, which oddly enough was named Downey Avenue. It was a small strip center consisting of a row of 4 or 5 shops with a small Pronto Market on the corner, which later became Trader Joe's. Next to the market was a boarded up, 1000 square foot, abandoned meat shop, which we regarded as our *golden opportunity*

We were overwhelmed by the stench of old meat that permeated the premises. The electricity was off and the place reeked from an old refrigerator that hadn't been cleaned for only God knew how long.

The landlord, Mr. Cummings, an elderly impeccably dressed man stood at the door... too smart to step one foot inside of this decomposing pit. He was very warm, engaging and supportive of our plans for this space which had nothing but a history of failures and had been empty for a long time.

He owned the building and had everything to gain from our success. Upon reflection, I think he liked our youthful enthusiasm and energy. Benny and I grabbed some cleaning supplies, mops, scrubbers and rags, and started cleaning the place from top to bottom. It went on for days.

Thanks to my mom and dad, I come from a family with a strong work ethic, but no matter how hard I worked Ben worked harder. I would get there at 7 a.m. and Ben had been there since 5 a.m. I quickly found out there were no shortcuts to small business. It is work, work, and more work. Finally after a few weeks with no pay, things were looking a lot cleaner and smelling a lot fresher. Our meat shop boasted fresh paint, clean windows and old but clean and functional antique display cases. Mr. Cummings owned several movie theaters and had extra carpet, so he installed new red wall to wall carpeting in the customer area to add a little class.

It was time to busy ourselves with putting together a strategy for a functioning meat shop and finding purveyors who would sell meats and provisions to two green horns with no credit. We decided to visit Manning Beef in Pico Rivera, a high quality meat company. They sold only the highest grade of meat and we hoped they would sell us. We obviously showed our inexperience in running a business but maybe they liked our attitude or enthusiasm, but whatever it was, it worked and they extended 7 day credit terms which meant we could get our delivery, sell the product and hopefully pay them their money in 7 days. We had made it over another hurdle.

In preparation for the opening day, I put the sign making skills I learned in Indiana from Mike Defabis to work. I picked out specials for our opening and plastering signs up to promote our new business. The big opening day was near.

Since we were dealing with perishable items, and freshness was very important, we received our meats and seafood, the day before we opened. We spent the day cutting, trimming, grinding and preparing our display cases. Bennie decided to put new fluorescent light bulbs in the display cases to make everything brighter. As he was installing the last bulb, I heard a loud pop and saw him grab his hand…he had a bad cut.

Everything came to a grinding halt, as we headed to the hospital to get him stitched up. So only hours before opening, Ben stood there with a bulky bandage wrapped around his hand. Not to be deterred, I finished the preparation, cleaned up and we headed home for a little sleep before the big event.

We arrived early and Ben didn't even mention his hand or complain of any pain. Our savior, Mr. Cummings, had the grand opening flags, balloons and, signs in place for the event. We were surprised, for we didn't have a clue how to do that. We managed to get all our display cases readied. Bennie's mom fixed her favorite anise cookies and brewed a big pot of Italian coffee.

We were only an hour from opening, and realized that we had given very little thought to the fact we not only had to cut and package the meats and price them, but we had to collect the money. There was an old fashioned cash register behind the counter that Ben and I knew absolutely nothing about. Someone ran down the street to the bank for some change and we had a five minute crash course in how to use a register. Did I say ignorance is bliss? I look back and remember being excited but not too nervous.

Downey was a pleasant city with a somewhat affluent population twelve miles from Los Angeles. Retired people living in apartments near our store would walk past our shop to do their daily shopping. Since they didn't eat much, the meat shop was great for them because they could order small portions. We could start out nice and easy. Good old Mr. Cummings had all his friends show up and buy meats, cheese, and seafood all day. It really helped build our confidence. At the end of the day we were exhausted but quite happy for the business we had done.

Day number one was behind us. We cleaned up, turned out the lights and stumbled out to the car for our long drive home. Bennie's injured hand? No problem, just another early lesson in business and how you have to keep moving and let the show go on. All the buildup and preparation for the big grand opening day was now behind us and it was time for day two and the future

CHAPTER 9

K-BOBS & CABBAGE ROLLS

It was quite a reality check when I realized our business would be open every day and we were responsible for its success or failure. We soon fell into a pattern of a day to day routine; clean, prep the foods, wait on customers, make sure everything was fresh, make special signs for windows and promotions and clean some more. We needed a crash course in Business 101. Not only were we meat cutters and order takers we had to be cashiers, accountants, advertiser/promoters, maintenance men, janitors and buyers.

Meanwhile, we had wives and families to provide for and obligations to meet. Thank God for the exuberance of youth. I recall the unbound energy that I had and the excitement of going to work and figuring out how to succeed in business. Obviously another facet of business is accounting. Our idea of accounting was to wait on customers, put the money in our big old time cash register....at the end of the day, count it, mark down our sales in a loose leaf note book and take the money to the bank every few days. Once a week we'd write checks to the few purveyors who were kind enough to give us credit, pay the electric bill and the rent. Then and only then, if anything was left we got paid.

There was very little left to pay ourselves. We were scraping by for that first year and when that meat started getting a little old after sitting there with no buyers, we would take it home. There was no filet mignon in our diet, but a lot of chuck roast and bones for soup. I didn't give it much thought for we were somehow surviving...barely.

It became apparent after a few months that this little meat shop could hardly support two families. I volunteered to take what skills I had and go to work at an all-night, 24 hour supermarket in West Covina called Thriftimart. I would report to work at 11 pm and was greeted with a long list of meat cutting chores; long enough to keep me busy all night.

The preparation room temperature was maintained at 36 degrees in order to keep the meats fresh and, hopefully, me awake. I would attack the long list of tasks and have the music blaring as I merrily worked away. All the time challenging myself and keeping a positive attitude while knocking out the list which kept getting longer and longer as the day manager saw that I could really turn out the work.

Little did I know he was taking advantage of my situation until I learned that he didn't expect that much out of others who worked that shift alone. The conditions of working in a 36 degree room all night were somewhat challenging. Maybe just moving around fast helped me deal with the cold, but on the other hand, the list became longer and longer.

Around 3 o'clock in the morning I would take a break and go into the *heated* break room for my *lunch*. The warmth really felt good, but the end result of warming up, especially at 3 o'clock in the morning was the wall I hit when my body was screaming... *sleep*. I would finish my *lunch* break...go back into the 36 degree cutting room, finish my shift and clean up the entire facility. At the end of the shift, I exited the store into a warm California morning and immediately feel the urge to fall asleep. Many a morning I would fall asleep in the car before attempting the drive home. Never work a grave shift If you don't have to especially in a dangerous environment with sharp knives and power saws... forget it! Nevertheless, I was thrilled to get an actual check from my night shift and be able to support my family. But, things were looking pretty bleak.

Meanwhile, back at the shop, Bennie was running the meat place as a one man show. Not only did he do all the preparation, sell, and package the meats, but he had the additional task of keeping the place clean and doing the banking. One thing he had going for him...he was a hell of a worker; an absolute must to make it in business. He often would get up at 4 am to drive the hour, to work and then run the place all day and drive all the way home only to repeat it the next day.

One problem we quickly realized with this strategy was we could not expect the business to survive and grow with only one man working. Many days, especially weekends, I would leave my night job and drive to Downey to help Ben on busier days. Certainly, I did it without much thought because I had a true burning desire to make it work as well.

This was the dilemma...what do we do now? Something needed to be done to grow the business or face the reality of giving up. Those long freeway drives back and forth to Downey gave me a lot of time to think.

I took a hard look at what our shop could offer that would differentiate us and create a greater appeal to generate more business. Why should customers come to us to buy their meat when they could go to a supermarket and get it for a better price?

The proverbial light went on in my head and I decided we needed some signature items that they could only get at Meralta Square Meat Shop...from good old Ben and Randy. We started making our own meat loaf mix; a combination of chopped vegetables and spices mixed into our fresh ground beef. We would tell the customer how to prepare this wonderful blend and take all the work out of it for them. Along with our meat loaf we offered stuffed bell peppers, stuffed pork chops, and even stuffed cabbage, which we prepared in our little cubby hole of an office as we delicately rolled our meat and veggie blend into cabbage rolls.

When we found ourselves staring at steaks that were still good but maybe a day or two old, we decided to cube the meat and marinate it in a spice sauce creation. We threaded the steak meat on wooden skewers to make shish-k-bobs. It was a thing of beauty to see our new look in our meat display. The steak-k-bobs were stacked high in the center. Then the fresh meat loaf mix and further down the line, the stuffed peppers, cabbage rolls and the stuffed pork chops. Then to make our meat display more unique we stopped at a mushroom farm in Santa Fe Springs on the way to work to buy fresh picked organic button mushrooms. We dumped them into a wicker basket in the center of our steak section which added a beautiful accent to the steak offerings. Before we knew it, we were selling all kinds of mushrooms.

We admired our display and I said, "Stack it high and watch it fly…Put it low, it will never go!" I used my sign making skills, to make a sign for each item and tell how wonderful it was. Of course no idea is going to work if you don't talk it up and explain to the customer the life changing experience they will have with your meat loaf or shish-ka-bob. Benny with his New York accent and good looks became quite the salesman. I never was shy myself with promoting a new idea and I think I quickly learned another Business 101 lesson; *believe in your product!*

The new items were a smashing success. We got to the shop early and loaded the pans a foot high. We happily talked the items up…gave the customer a card on how to prepare the item...and sent them on their way. The response was overwhelming with all positive comments.

We quickly became aware that offering the various items made us unique. Something as simple as stopping at an egg ranch in Pomona and buying dozens of fresh brown eggs to stack on the counter became a staple. Bennie's mom made the famous Italian Pasta Fagioli soup that we sold by the quart. And the best part…with the increase in business I could quit my night job cutting meat and rejoin Ben at the meat shop…maybe we would make it!

All the new signature items were selling well and it became a challenge to freshly prep everything, especially on Saturday mornings. But by the time we opened, we had built stacks and stacks of the offerings and then began the job of talking it up to sell them. But as time went on re realized most of the sales had become repeat customers sales. We knew that in order to support two families we had to keep growing the business and attracting new customers.

We were suddenly moving toward Catering 101. When a customer asked if we catered, at first I didn't know what she was talking about. She explained, "You know, fix food platters and salads for a party or wedding reception." Initially, I turned her down but a light went on in my head. The next morning I retrieved the yellow pages and looked under catering and proceeded to call different companies. I pretend I was having a company meeting for say…100 people, or sometimes I would pretend I had a daughter getting married and was planning a reception for 200.

When they went into the sales pitch I would begin writing feverishly to get the information on paper. I would ask as many questions as I could until I felt they were talked out. So we had some nice signs made up about our party platters and the wide variety of meats, cheeses and salads from which to choose. We put together ideas for relish platters and salads, and whatever other ideas I had garnered from my fake phone calls to other caterers. The fall of the year had arrived and we were hoping to do some holiday business…we were keenly aware and extra receptive to anything that may have led to a catering opportunity.

CHAPTER 10

HAPPY THANKSGIVING

I received an inquiry from a customer who asked if we cooked turkeys for Thanksgiving. I paused for a second and stammered out, "Yes." I told her I would have all the details tomorrow. Quickly, I fumbled through recipe books and figured what a basic Thanksgiving dinner could be. I came up with a whole baked turkey with all the trimmings, including dressing, mashed potatoes, gravy, etc. I think the whole package was maybe $15.95.

Obviously we weren't up to snuff on markup percentages and surely could have charged substantially more but we were always so flattered and thrilled to death to have any business. We did have enough sense to run an ad in the local paper. The phone started ringing off the hook and before we knew it we had 10 orders, then 20 orders, 30, 50, 75. We got a little scared. Where do we stop? Before we knew it we had

114 orders and we said that's it! One slight detail…we didn't even own an oven. We jumped in the car and went to LA in search of an oven. One problem was that we were meat cutters not chef and had no idea about ovens and real restaurant equipment…two rookies with no experience buying ovens. We made our way to Los Angeles St., the street known for restaurant equipment wholesalers. We just wandered into the first place we saw. It wasn't long before we parted with the nest egg we had been squirreling away. We were proud owners of a Black Monster two deck oven. Being from the Midwest I was sure the salesman was a wonderfully honest guy who wouldn't dream of unloading some out of date, dust collector black oven that he had sitting in his backroom for years. It never even crossed my mind that there were stainless steel ovens.

In short, Ben and I made space for the black monster in the backroom of the meat shop hooked up the gas and were quite proud when it actually worked. We had just taken our first step at becoming Chefs. Or so we thought, I guess it might be referred to as baptism by fire. We had 114 turkeys to cook and had never cooked a thing, let alone a turkey. I remember thinking if that oven breaks down we are dead!" there are 115 families waiting for two rank amateurs to prepare their most important meal of the year.

What had we gotten ourselves into? I remember having to convince myself to stay positive…stay cool and that I could do it. Who was I kidding? Ben and I also realized we needed to sell quality products to set us apart from chain store meat counters. For that reason we searched out Shelton turkey farm up in Carbon Canyon near Brea, California. Mr. Shelton was an older gentleman who raised perfect free range organic turkeys and was real picky who he sold to. I told him how I had been on my family's farm in the Midwest and how we raised chickens and hunted wild turkeys...*a real stretch*. His parents had been from Indian. I shared my love for a famous state park in Indiana called Turkey Run State Park. He had been there. Whatever the conversation took to convince him we were worthy of selling his wonderful turkeys in our little meat market in Downey. He finally had warmed up to us when he saw how excited we were to be considered worthy enough to sell his turkeys. He finally asked how many we thought we could sell. For some reason I blurted out 300. He seemed surprised. We shook hands and off we went to figure out not only how to cook 114 turkeys but how to sell an additional 200.

I remember my mom and those fabulous homemade Indiana country style meals. Especially Thanksgiving. There's nothing like a mom's cooking; the mashed potatoes, the perfect gravy, green beans seasoned with bacon, and the dressing...how could I forget the dressing? I thought it was time to call my mom and refresh my memory.

All I remember about her cooking and Thanksgiving in particular was eating myself into oblivion, then collapsing on the sofa, followed up and hour or two later to eat my way to Kokomo and back on her unbelievable pies; cherry, banana cream, butterscotch, and her tasty bread pudding.

It brought me to tears to remember my mom's meals and how positive and supporting she was of me no matter what mischief I got into. I called her for a crash course in how to cook Thanksgiving dinner. But hearing and doing is two different things, as any *chef* will tell you. Too bad I didn't pay attention when my mom made gravy.

When we posted our sign as official organic Shelton Turkey sellers, the orders for the turkeys for people to buy and cook themselves picked up dramatically. We not only had sold 200 fresh turkeys but had the commitment to cook 114 additional turkey dinners to be picked up Thanksgiving Day. Ben and I looked at each other in amazement, scared, but certainly thrilled to have all that business. Pushed to the limit was an understatement because at that age 24 and new to business, we had no clue to our limits. Therefore, we devised a plan; let's see…we can cook 16 turkeys at once in our *Big Bertha* oven. It takes 4 hours, hmmm…doing the math the numbers just didn't add up. We needed more oven space.

Bennie and I went down the street to a little German deli/restaurant for breakfast some mornings. Hilda and Ingrid; two very staunch, strict and to the point Germans ran the little operation. They overheard us talking about our dilemma and much to our surprise volunteered to cook some turkeys in their oven and even take some to cook at home. Great! God bless Germany! This could've been our out…we not only enlisted the Germans we had other volunteers to cook a few; family, friends, strangers, we didn't care…we were feeling the heat…literally.

We went to the day-old bakery and bought loaves of bread to chop up for dressing, the celery, onions, eggs, spices were added. Let's see! What else did my mom tell me? Pots of chicken wings and seasoning were simmering to create a rich broth to use in the gravy. The camp style little stoves weren't ideal but they worked. What about the green beans, and mashed potatoes?

This was all going on while Bennie and I were working our meat counter the day before Thanksgiving. The Shelton turkeys, hams and prime ribs, were being weighed, packaged, carried out to the car.

We were in a frenzy…busy mixing and stuffing these magnificent birds with dressing. We made a schedule and shoved the first 16 birds in our old *Big Bertha* oven. The Germans took theirs to cook as did the other volunteers. It was a flurry of activity with no time for errors. Finally around 7 pm Bennie went home to get some sleep and promised to come back early the next morning. If we had any chance of pulling this off I had to spend the night reloading the ovens every 4 hours, basting and turning the turkeys and finish preparing the side dishes. We didn't have an exhaust fan and the place reeked of turkeys cooking and steam filled the shop. I just swung the doors open to get some fresh air and kept on moving. It smelled good to me! About 3 a.m., I looked up to see Bennie standing there; as he handed me a cup of coffee and told me to go get a few hours sleep and come back in the morning. Thank heaven for Ben and his insomnia. I went home to Pomona, still unsure we could pull this off.

Bennie might have had insomnia, but I was just the opposite. Once I hit the pillow, I was out like a light. Good in some ways, not always wise when you're preparing Thanksgiving dinner for probably 500 people. I rolled over about 8:30 the next morning trying to come to my senses and remembered what I had to do that day. When it hit me that I had overslept I was up like a flash and behind the wheel driving like a maniac to Downey an hour away! I couldn't believe I was going to let Ben down like this.

When I pulled into the parking lot there were cars everywhere. I didn't know whether to go in the shop to face a lot of mad customers wanting to pick up their Thanksgiving dinners. What a joke this idea was, I thought as I walked slowly to the front doors ready to accept the wrath of my misdeeds. To say I was totally surprised is a big understatement. The front doors were propped wide open; the place was impeccably clean, music playing, fresh made Italian cookies lined the counter to go along with the pot of coffee. I mean when I left that place the night before it was a disaster. Turns out Bennie and his wife Lia knew a thing or two about cooking. The orders were neatly wrapped, marked and lined all the counter tops. The side dishes were deliciously prepared and ready to go.

After I got over the initial shock, I naturally helped finish with the order distribution; Ben really came through and how could I ever thank the turkey roasting volunteers who had seen two young, eager, inexperienced guys who were in over their heads and needed a hand. Just goes to prove that no matter how good an idea is, if you can't pull it off...it is worthless. I might add that we had nothing but rave reviews on those 114 turkeys we prepared. Thank you Lord.

Finally, Thanksgiving was behind us. Now we were ready for the next challenge. Our successful Thanksgiving was a boost to our confidence to say the least. Christmas was fast approaching and with our new catering signs and faith in ourselves we were getting orders for our party platters.

Through trial and error and after a day of browsing recipes and party planning books at the Pomona Library I could put together a decent looking meat tray or relish tray. Again to our surprise, we started getting orders for small company parties and events. We were so busy we had to pull an all-night shift on December 23 to be ready for all the platters for Christmas Eve. Again we did it. Thank God we didn't get sick or break a leg. I do remember being exhausted…driving home and falling into my big easy chair. I recall my 9-day-old son Randy in my arms as I fell asleep. I was doubly thankful!

CHAPTER 11

YES…WE DO

We made it past the holiday season and were surprised at the success of our new found revenue source from catering. With our *can do* attitude we had managed to stumble through the party tray business and even managed some nice compliments. Our confidence had picked up significantly. Along with our youthful energy level and naiveté we were ready for any catering challenge, or so we thought. For the first time we were asked if we catered weddings. Of course the answer was, "Yes…we do."

An older couple owned a small print shop close by on Firestone Ave. The wife stopped by the shop to pick up a chuck roast occasionally and was willing to trade meat for printing. So they were willing to put a brochure together touting our wonderful catering services and all it cost us was a lifetime supply of chuck roast for Flo and Bob. It sounded like a good deal to me. It was time to once again call the real catering companies and pretend I was getting married. I pumped as much information as I could and feverishly took notes. Flo and Bob printed a nice brochure describing how wonderful we were and all of our services. However, we did not really have a clue as to how to pull it off if heaven forbid we actually landed a job.

We named our *new venture* Camelot Catering, and even went so far as to put a phone line in for all the calls we expected as caterers. We had the bright idea to pass by the Downey Presbyterian Church nearby to see if they were having any wedding receptions in their social hall. As luck would have it, they were having a reception that Saturday so Ben and I wore our suits to work that day and proceeded to crash the reception to see a real caterer in action. We edged our way into the side door and walked around with big smiles acting like we were supposed to be there. All the while, we were seeing how the food and tables were set up and how the whole event went off. Actually, I am ashamed to say we grabbed a plate and went through the line. The potato salad was pretty good but Ben swore ours was better. After a quick handshake with the groom we made a hasty exit before our undercover mission was exposed.

Soon after our spying mission, the *hot line* phone rang. Nervously I answered the phone with all the trembling confidence in the world..."Camelot Catering". Some ladies daughter was getting married and they were interested in us possibly catering the event. I must have sounded half-way convincing with my rehearsed sales pitch, because they booked an appointment to come by their house to discuss the details. So a few days later, armed with my new and empty briefcase; a prop to make me look important, I showed up at their door to discuss the big event. I can't remember what I said during that first encounter and I was fighting my inner desire to run, but the husband and wife must have liked my price, which I am sure, was ridiculously cheap. Maybe they had too many martinis, but they agreed to let us cater the reception.

We were excited to get a chance to do a real catering job. We probably would have done it for free. Finally the Saturday arrived for our first *big gig*. I recall the sleepless night before and hoping I was sharp enough the next day to pull it off. As usual, Ben beat me to the shop and was way ahead of the day's work. We had made a list of preparations and made sure we had everything clean and ready to go. I decided to drive down to the hall and check the layout and see where we could park. Upon my return to the shop, I was relieved to see that Ben's wife, Lia, had arrived to lend us a hand.

Lia had a charming personality that could really help cover our mistakes. The client had also asked us to provide a punch for the reception…*no problem*…that's what a real *experienced* caterer would have said. I checked with the hair stylist next door to our meat shop and she told me how she made her punch for her wedding. Armed with this *special punch recipe*, I had all the ingredients ready to mix. We would make one with champagne and one non-alcoholic. I asked Lia to bring her retired father, Joe Vitale to be the bartender. Joe, a handsome man in his own right, with perfect wavy silver hair and impeccably dressed in a three piece silk suit with handkerchief would have looked more at home as a Maitre d' at the Four Season's Hotel in New York City where he had lived before moving West to join his daughter. Maybe a little overdressed for the punch dipping job but, none the less, he was much appreciated. He gave our operation some class. Obviously, Joe wanted us to succeed and was a good sport about his assignment.

The hour was fast approaching. There were 200 guess who were depending on us to feed them and the thought of failing didn't even enter my mind. It became a mind game and a real test of our confidence. The actual quantity of food to prepare was a big worry. We figured the biggest mistake we could make was to run out of food, so we made sure we had extra.

Benny ran out to the parking lot to retrieve his big family Oldsmobile station wagon to begin loading the food. After turning the key and grinding away, there was no response…Luck was with us…we ran into the hair salon next door and they gave us jumper cables to fire up the big V8 engine. We had lost fifteen or twenty minutes but we were still in the game. We loaded the station wagon to the brim with our meat, cheese, relish trays, breads, punches, and utensils. We tore out of the parking lot, down Downey Ave. in a blur to meet our destiny in the wonderful world of catering. The adrenalin was pumping! We pulled up to the back door and started unloading the food with a fury. The tablecloths were all in place and beautiful centerpieces graced each table. Let's see…the tableware goes here…the breads here, meat trays here…I thought out loud as I surveyed the layout.

The cake table was off to the side and the baker had just

made his entrance with his master piece. We had nothing to do with the cake...thank God they didn't ask me about a cake or I probably would have tried to provide that too in my eagerness to get the job. The baker had the three layers in place and was just putting the final layer on. Just as he was placing the top layer I noticed that one end of the table was slowly folding down and the cake was starting to slide to the floor. I was about ten feet away and what followed seemed like it was in slow motion as I dived for the cake to break the fall. The front of my *Sunday go to church* suit was covered with pink icing but I had managed to keep the accident from being a total disaster. The baker was nearly in tears as he scooped up the damaged cake and hustled it behind the stage to work some magic.

He couldn't thank me enough for my *heroic action*. I stood there with icing from top to bottom, but nothing a damp towel couldn't clean up as I hurriedly wiped my suit. Luckily the baker had some repair icing on hand to do a quick touch up. The cause of the table giving away was the fact that whoever set the tables up that morning had not locked the table legs in place with the slide latches. I quickly looked to see that the table legs on our buffet tables were locked and in place. A lesson learned and to this day I check to see that any portable tables I use have the legs properly secured.

I proceeded to mix the punch with champagne and the separate bowl for those who preferred no alcohol. As I was briefing Joe on how to ladle the punch and serve it, I remembered to slow down my speech to make sure he understood. When I was nervous I spoke too fast, and Joe with his native Italian language just stared at me as I blabbered away as fast as I could. Finally everything was in place...the buffet looked great, the cake was repaired; the people were starting to go to the buffet. Lia played her role as she graciously handed plates to the guest. Time was passing and the guests were hitting the buffet hard. Our foresight to have extra food out in the station wagon was brilliant as we used most everything. They particularly liked the potato salad. I finally got around to checking on Joe. There was a cluster of teenagers and preteens in front of his punch station who were in a crush to get more of his tasty punch. I noticed they were quite loud and seemed to be having a lot of fun. Empty champagne bottles littered the floor behind the table as he tried to keep up with the demand. As I was observing his dilemma, I noticed he was giving the alcoholic champagne punch to the kids by mistake. I guess my instructions got lost in translation.

The non-alcohol punch was being given to the adults. No wonder these kids were having so much fun! Earlier when I was explaining to Joe that the kids received the punch from the non-alcoholic bowl he became confused with my English as I spoke too fast and was just doing his best to keep up. Well after correcting the misunderstanding, it was a little late as the kids were having a great time dancing and running wild. I quickly realized it was time for us to gather our dishes, platters and utensils and make a hasty exit stage left. We had survived our first real catering adventure!

Lesson learned! The 7 P's...Prior Proper Planning Prevents Piss Poor Performance.

CHAPTER 12

HOLY PASTRAMI

The extra revenue from catering was helping keep the doors open but catering was somewhat seasonal and we needed an increase in day to day sales to keep going. We each took a bare bones salary and once in a while a little extra if we had a good catering order. We were always thinking of new ideas to keep us going. We didn't necessarily have to worry about starving to death in a sense. We had a full display case of meat. As the display would age we merely took the outdated or brownish looking items home to feed our families.

We knew the importance of keeping our display looking fresh and appetizing. It was the accumulation of too many roasts to sell or take home to eat that was somewhat a turning point of our career. The idea was hatched to take these aged but slightly outdated cuts and slowly roast them in our oven in a spice mixture that we threw together. Since we had fresh loaves of Italian bread being delivered from Galasso's Baker, we asked Vinney, our driver, to bring us some long sandwich rolls. We sliced the cooked meats very thin and simmered the meat in its natural juice that we saved while roasting. We had just bought a piece of a cured meat with which I was unfamiliar, called pastrami. Being from Indiana, bologna, ham and pickle loaf was about as exotic as it got for us.

Pastrami was a beef cut that was cured in pepper and came from the front quarter had a nice grain of fat running through it to give it a terrific flavor as it was heated. We also sliced the pastrami thin and simmered it in natural juices, Ben and I sliced opened a flakey fresh Italian roll and piled some juicy sliced roast beef on one and then made a pastrami sandwich to try. I don't know what we did or a combination of everything coming together but the flavor was of another world…maybe the old world. We sliced a kosher pickle from the barrel of pickles we had just received from A-1 Eastern Pickle Company in Los Angeles.

The crispy crunch of the pickle and the sandwich were just the ticket. It was still morning and I stepped into the backroom and knocked out a couple of signs and posted them on the front door proclaiming that we were in the sandwich business. Notjust any sandwich…our original slow roasted *roast beef* or *pastrami sandwich* served on a fresh baked Italian roll. We priced them at $1.50 each. We excited and anxious to see if anyone would order one and what their reaction would be when they bit into it. Could this be the solution to getting rid of the outdated cuts of meat that we were looking for? As the lunch hour approached we did in fact sell four sandwiches.

I'm sure people found it a little strange that we were selling sandwiches in a meat market. The next day we sold a few more and each day a few more as the word spread. With our limited inexperience in the restaurant business we weren't concerned about portion control so we really piled the meat on. We loaded up the oven with beef roasts in the morning and as they roasted we propped the front doors open to get some air in the place. As the wonderful smells floated around the downtown area, it became our best advertisement.

When lunch time approached we frantically assembled the sandwiches as they were ordered. We quickly tore off a sheet of white butcher paper, threw in a quartered crunchy kosher pickle and wrapped the sandwich in a flash. It became a real diversion when a customer came in to purchase something from the fresh meat side of the small shop. We could hardly wait to get them out fast enough to get back over to our sandwich rush. Ben and I had a new found sense that we were on to something. We got excited as we happily prepped for the onslaught each morning. We began to realize that we had a solution for staying afloat, and at last, giving us some breathing room. My sleepless nights of wondering if we could make it in business were quickly becoming how to keep up with the increased business.

As it turned out, our location in the downtown area of Downey worked out to be a major plus for us. With a limited number of residence downtown it was tough to make it operating as a traditional meat market. But as a sandwich operation with all the store fronts, offices and even the courts nearby, the word spread quickly.

Every day at lunch there was a line of office workers, attorneys, and business men waiting for one of our special sandwiches...it was special to us. We had zero experience in the restaurant business so we were flying by the seat of our pants. I still remember the nervousness of the lunch rushes making sandwiches and learning to work together as a team.

We were so busy we just piled the cash up in a box rather than ring it on a register, which took too much time. The prices were rounded to the quarter so we didn't mess with nickels, dimes or pennies. At the end of the rush, dollar bills were overflowing the box and falling to the floor. What a wonderful problem! To say our accounting methods were crude would be an understatement. We didn't know much about terms such as gross profit; cost of goods sold, and portion control...all we knew was that we were busy as hell and the sandwiches were flying out the door.

If we didn't have enough to keep up with the roast beef and pastrami sandwiches, we started a steak sandwich just for the fun of it. We trimmed and ran, what was a largely unknown skirt steak, through a meat tenderizing machine to create a thin steak that was about 3 inches by 12 inches long. We found an old grill to quickly flash broil the cut. The meat would literally be hanging out the ends of the crispy Italian roll with Best Foods mayonnaise, fresh sliced tomato and lettuce. It was terrific!

It became a hit and keeping up with the demand got to be somewhat comical with flames shooting up as we worked through the orders. I had a flash back to Frank and Mary's tavern and the hellish rushes that I would sit and watch, all the while being entertained by their banter as they struggled to keep up with the pork tenderloin sandwich business.

I began to see how the business could become addicting; not for just the money, but for the pleasure of creating an idea...seeing it work and the high of riding the wave of the rush and the satisfaction when it was over. There was also the camaraderie of working together as a team and doing the job and the appreciation of the customers who seemed to feel they were a part of the success. I understood Frank and Mary's enjoyment as the popularity of their sandwich grew and became the talk of the town. I think that little wink and smile Frank would give Mary once in a while had a lot more meaning than the simple gesture. Possible he was saying, "Can you believe this? I found myself asking Bennie the same question.

With the amount of business we had established we were presented with a new problem. We needed employees. As if on cue, straight out of Central Casting, a teenager named Jerry Meador walked in looking for a part time job. He was an All-American looking kid with a quick and friendly smile...we hired him on the spot. As turned to walk away, he stopped and asked if we needed more help. He said his brother was looking for a job, too. I said, "Sure bring him with you. What's his name?"

"Larry" he replied.

"Okay Jerry and Larry sounds good to me."

On Saturday morning, the brothers reported to work. Much to my amazement they were identical twins with identical voices. They stood there with white shirts and aprons...it was impossible to tell them apart. They turned out to be fabulous workers.

They were from a Mormon family and were a testament to the goodness and wholesomeness of their upbringing. It was quite a novelty as customers became confused while they waited on them and thought they were seeing double...it was always good for a big laugh.

CHAPTER 13

ABALONE FOR SALE

Downey, California, had a diverse population. With L.A. being just down the road, it had a mix of some pretty well-healed citizens in addition to a lot of working class average people. John Rush, a free spirited customer of our fine establishment was neither well-healed nor average. He came to Downey to visit his mom, but actually lived on a boat at the marina in Long Beach. While he would be wolfing down a roast beef sandwich he would share with us his diving adventures off of Catalina Island. As I listened to him it was pretty intriguing stuff for someone from Indiana. The only experience of anything connected to the ocean while living in landlocked Indiana was what I had seen on T. V. There I was talking to a guy who lives on a boat and goes out diving.

John told us of this wonderful shellfish creature he would dive for called an abalone. The only fish I knew about growing up were catfish or maybe bass and blue gill caught from a lake. Abalone sure sounded exotic to me. One day, John was nice enough to bring us an abalone. It was a giant sea snail or mollusk about the size of a softball. He removed it from the shell and trimmed off the outside covering. After slicing it paper thin, he pounded the portions out with a mallet and dipped the abalone steaks in eggs beaten with salt and pepper and then into a bread crumb mixture. The steaks were then quickly pan seared in a skillet of hot butter and olive oil for one minute on each side. What a delicacy! Very unique taste! The best part was that John was getting them by the basket.

John loved our roast beef dip sandwich and with the potential to sell these abalone things maybe we could do some business. So we traded abalone for sandwiches. We had installed a showcase with fresh fish for sale and where else could you buy abalone just off the boat. Ben had experience with fish and would drive into Los Angeles to the American Fish Company and buy the fresh fish for our shop. He would build a beautiful iced display and have it loaded to the brim with *today's catch*. Just another thing we hoped would make our place different.

It never entered our mind that our little meat shop was becoming too diversified. We not only sold meats, cold cuts, cheeses and salads, but we did catering and ran a full sandwich shop operation. We now offered live lobsters, fresh fish and abalone and all this in a thousand square foot space. We were excited and having fun, but obviously oblivious to our limits. Our old friend John Rush would call us from the dock then go out diving to fill our order. One afternoon he walked in with a bag of fresh abalone.

We were having a good time selling abalone for around five or six dollars a pound. John was getting fatter and fatter gobbling down our sandwiches and we were selling a lot of abalone. The supply was bountiful and there were few restrictions. John was able to supply such large quantities, that I got the bright idea to run an ad in the *Penny Shopper Newspaper*. We prepared the abalone and froze it in two pound packages to sell for some ridiculous price. We sure didn't have trouble selling all that John could provide. Today, abalone sells for over $50.00 a pound and is very hard to find.

All was going quite well, until one day a gentleman walked in and asked if he could buy some of that abalone he had seen advertised in the *Penny Shopper* newspaper. To our surprise after he paid for the abalone he pulled out a badge and announced he was a game warden from the California Fish and Game Department. He proceeded to write us a ticket for selling fish from a non-inspected source. Not only that, but he confiscated all of our abalone! It appeared that our enthusiasm for the business was getting us into a lot of trouble! We didn't have a clue that we were doing something illegal?

A few weeks later, we were more than nervous as we made our way down the street to the courthouse to appear on the charges. I guess it never even entered our mind to hire an attorney to represent us. We stood dressed in our Sunday suits before a judge at the Downey courthouse. The judge regularly came into our shop blocks just a few block from the courthouse to buy sandwiches. The game warden quoted a statute that he had used to site us. The judge asked our side of the story. We stammered around as we told him we had bought it from a licensed diver. The judge paused as he read the law.

After a few minutes he proceeded to tell the game warden he found the wording vague and since we were buying from a licensed diver, he didn't see any law we had broken. He reprimanded the warden for finding some obscure law that interfered with these two fine young men trying to make a living in their small business. *Case Dismissed!*

All days at the shop weren't always so serious. After all we were pretty young guys and joked around to keep things light and have a little fun along the way. I think this attitude helped us keep our sanity until we found a formula that worked for our business.

The small strip center we occupied was anchored on one end by Pronto Market. There was a hair salon and a few offices next to us and at the other end was a restaurant spot that had just switched from a coffee shop to a Chinese restaurant.

Like us, the Wong family would arrive at work early in the morning to prepare for the day's business. They pretty much kept to themselves and occasionally would wave back to us as we said good morning. One day as I was taking out the trash, I heard some strange sounds coming from the rear of the Chinese restaurant. As I walked toward their back door I discovered the source of the strange noises. Tied up with twine just outside their door were three plump chickens strutting around and enjoying the morning sun, obviously unaware of their certain doom. I am not always that sharp in the morning, but I quickly figured out what the Wong's used for that famous chicken soup. Why else would three live chickens be tied up behind the restaurant? I couldn't believe in this day and age that live birds would be used. I walked back in the shop and told Ben and the Meador twins of the livestock wandering around in our alley.

Opposed to minding our own business this sure looked like an opportunity for a prank. I picked up the phone and called the Chinese restaurant. They put me on hold until they found the only person who spoke English. I told him I was with the Los Angeles County Health Department and I understood they have live chickens behind their restaurant. "We know you have been using these in your kitchen," I added. "We need to confiscate them and run some tests. Please bring the chickens to the corner of Downey Avenue and 4th St. We will send someone to pick them up," I instructed.

To our amazement within ten minutes, we looked out our front door to see two Wong brothers, with their chef coats and tall white hats, walking the chickens very patiently down the sidewalk past our shop to Downey Ave. Of course we were laughing uncontrollable…forgetting it was at someone else's expense.

After about thirty minutes of their waiting on the corner we decided to call the restaurant once again to tell them the pickup was delayed and requested they take the chickens across the street to the Edison building, which it just so happened was in the direct line of sight from our front windows. I instructed them to tie the chickens up in the lobby. Several minutes went by until we spotted one of the brothers run by our window to relay the new message. Again, to our surprise the two brothers with the three chickens on the twine leash calmly crossed Downey Ave. to the Edison building.

They hesitated as they swung open the door and led the three birds inside the lobby. To our surprise they exited the lobby without the chickens and mad a bee-line back across Downey Avenue, past our windows and to the safety of their restaurant. Needless to say…chicken soup was not on the menu that day.

CHAPTER 14

CALIFORNIA DREAMIN'

Back in Indiana we clustered around the TV in the grip of winter on a cold blustery New Year's Day and watched the Rose Parade from Pasadena California and people running around in the sunshine wearing T-shirts, smiling and having a good time.

Fast forward and there I was right in the middle of Southern California, actually experiencing firsthand the California sites and action that I had only seen on a grainy television. Not only was I living the good California life, but I had the good fortune of meeting up with Benny and getting a chance to be in business.

We had hung in there, caught some lucky breaks and were still standing. The energy, exuberance of youth and I think the downright terror of failing had carried us to that point. As I look back, being naive certainly played a big part and not being overly educated was, in a way, an advantage because some of the seat of the pants choices and risk taking moments wouldn't have succeeded if we were making more educated and calculated decisions.

We were not reaping a lot of financial reward but that really was not much of consideration as bazaar as that might sound. We had made a big comeback and had turned our first venture around. It was a major accomplishment that we were paying our bills and taking home a salary. The independence of being your own boss was addicting. Even though I never became hooked on tobacco or alcohol and didn't know addiction first hand, there was a yearning for more of that business stuff. On the other hand, Ben may have been looking at things a little differently than I. He was older, and had four kids. I'm sure he was wondering at what point he should bail on some of the craziness and go get a real job. He was more quiet and introspective than I. Make no mistake about it he was a hell of a worker and had a wonderful personality and together we were making it happen.

But where were we going from there? The meat market was doing well for its size and limitations and we were having a lot of fun but it was time to do some serious thinking. My dad had told me that sometimes a day of thinking was better than a week of hard work. I wanted more of that California dream! Driving the hour plus to work and back was really getting to be a drag as the demands of business grew. It did have one side benefit and that was it provided a lot of time for reflection and for this thinking thing my dad had always talked about.

Being in my twenties I certainly wasn't at any mellowing

out stage, but I did realize we needed to make a move. The concept of a new business was rolling around in my mind. It sure did not include lugging around those heavy quarters of beef and doing traditional meat cuttings with the, trimming, grinding and labor intensive struggle to keep a fresh display for sale. The markup was very slim. Besides, you certainly could not compete with super markets, who if for no other reason could always beat you on price.

Delicatessen…a fascinating word if you really closed your eyes and thought about it. Could you smell the fresh breads stacked on the counter, see the wheels of cheese and the salami hanging from the ceiling? A display case busting at the seams with delicious salads, exotic meats and all the other tasty morsels you could imagine. Pastries? Sure only the best! Wines and pasta…why not? That was my vision. Strangely enough there really was not much of that in Southern California, at least not where we lived.

I remembered working with the Defabis brothers in Indiana .The delicatessen department in Brownsburg was very successful and it really didn't have the exotic meats cheeses that I had envisioned. Exotic at that time was basically bologna, pickle loaf, Colby cheese or maybe ham salad which is really a sandwich spread, not a salad…ham salad was an Indiana thing and I could turn out a mean one! We also had baked pies and the cream pies that were to die for.

In downtown Indianapolis there was Shapiro's Deli that was well known for their Jewish style corned beef sandwich. It sure felt good to walk in there and get engulfed in the atmosphere and for certain a corned beef on rye. I couldn't see all the details of our delicatessen, and the more I thought about it, I knew this was the direction to go. Hardly able to sleep, I drove to Downey the next morning. Ben and I hurriedly set up the meat case and then our usual break. We walked across Downey Ave. for breakfast at the German's, as we jokingly called them. I could hardly wait to spill my guts to Ben about this vision I had.

Speaking to Ben of the Delicatessen and the meats, salads, bread...the smells. The colors...the wines...Oh my God! The more I talked about it, the more excited I became and actually started believing myself. Was he listening? He was slowly eating his breakfast and glancing up at me.

Then something came to me. Wait a minute...this guy was from New York...Italian...Delicatessen...hell yes he knows what I envision. I blurted out It would have that old world look just like you remember in New York. We can even call it Old World Delicatessen if you want. I finally slowed down to catch my breath as Ben methodically put his fork down across the plate. He paused for what seemed like forever. He looked up at me and said three words, "Let's do it!" I nearly feel off my chrome bar stool at the counter. How is that for making an educated decision! Not much debate or talk about how we could pull this off. The reality of easier said than done was of little concern to us. After a few hours passed we started to figure what needed to be done. First of all we had to (1) sell or walk away from our meat shop (2) find a location for our dream delicatessen (3) design and put together the new venture. And with very limited funds and the need of a paycheck each week the timing was going to be pretty tricky. First things first...we had to keep an eye out for a possible location. We wanted it close to home or at least reasonably close. Then another factor was to find a developer or owner that would give us a lease and trust us to pay the rent…easier said than done.

A month or two went by and no luck. We were getting anxious until Ben took a short cut home to say hi to his cousin in the West Covina area. While driving down Azusa Ave., he spotted a sign in a shopping center about space for rent. It was in a hilly section of West Covina and was currently being developed as Woodside Village. The area homes were just being built and the center and its tenants were just surviving until the new homes were completed and occupied.

Unfortunately the space that was now empty was from a small Chinese fast food guy who couldn't hang on anymore and decided to walk out on the lease. Not an ideal location but the kind of gamble we would have to take to get an opportunity to try out our idea. We didn't consider demographics or any of that kind of mumble jumble…we just wanted a shot. So we picked up the phone and called Eichenbaum Properties in Beverly Hills. At least they answered the phone and were willing to talk to us. They said a representative could come by and speak to us at our meat shop in Downey. I was impressed they would drive all the way to Downey to check us out.

A few days later, this young guy in his early twenties walks in. He was good-looking, had a big smile, was nicely dressed, super friendly, outgoing and with an over the top positive attitude. He reminded me of Lois Lane's newspaper sidekick on the super man series. What was his name?

Jimmie Olson? He gave us a hearty handshake and introduced himself as Steven Soboroff. Turns out Steve was just finishing his studies at UCLA and had landed an internship with Eichenbaum Properties and was checking out what kind of idea we had for the vacant West Covina space. He seemed impressed with our little operation in Downey, or so we thought. He listened intently as we played out our plans. Maybe he was just acting. We did seem to connect and had a good conversation. Steve said his goodbyes and told us he would get back to us.

The next day we received a call from him saying he would like for us to come to Beverly Hills to meet Mr. Eichenbaum. Beverly Hills! Man that's a long way from Brownsburg Indiana! The next morning we jumped in Ben's old station wagon and headed down the 10 freeway toward LA and Beverly Hills. We had the maps in hand along with scribbled directions on a piece of butcher paper. We just hoped we wouldn't get lost on our way to this fateful meeting. I had seen Beverly Hills on TV from the series Beverly Hillbillies, but I glanced up and saw the HOLLYWOOD sign on the hills and just about fell out of the car. Was this for real? I began to wonder if we were way out of our league. Steve spotted us driving around in the parking lot of this beautiful high rise building and told us where to park. As we walked into the lobby of this first-class building, Steve explained to us where exactly to sit when we arrived at the office. He gave us suggestions on what to say and how to act toward Mr. E…as he referred to him. You could tell that he was just as nervous as we were about this meeting. At least, we had enough sense to brush off our suits and wear them. I sensed we were about to meet the president or something. The big doors opened and we found ourselves in this huge palatial space all decorated to the max, a beautiful bar to one side and a floor to ceiling window view of Beverly Hills. It would have made a perfect post card. At the center of the room was a raised area with a huge, beyond belief, ornate gorgeous desk. Seated behind the desk was his majesty himself. A small statured, tan and exceptionally well maintained, impeccably dressed 70ish man. He stood and introduced himself as Joseph Eichenbaum. Even with my youthful naiveté, I wondered what this guy was doing meeting with a couple of struggling butcher boys from our neck of the woods.

We took our assigned seats, just as Steve had coached us to do. I felt like we were at the base of the king's throne. We kept our mouths shut. It made no sense to me, but what did we have to loose. Mr. E was a very articulate, well-spoken interesting man and between quizzing us about our plan he seemed more interested in sharing with us his first entrepreneur venture as a young man.

He related how he had come across the enzyme powder of a papaya and through a few experimentations in his kitchen he had discovered by soaking meat in his potion that he had mixed, the steak would be tender. He had stumbled onto meat tenderizer and a marinade. It was certainly awe inspiring listening to him tell how he had bought a cement mixer and set it in the back of his brother's dry cleaner's business in Santa Monica. He proceeded to mix the ingredients and package the product for sale. The name of the product was Adolph's Meat Tenderizer and Marinade. It became popular beyond his wildest expectations. The idea had made him a wealthy man. I still remember the excitement in his voice and the passion and disbelief he spoke of as he related the story.

Maybe he could feel our passion, as he did as a young man in the belief and excitement of a new idea. I do remember it was real special to be sitting there as he shared his personal journey to succeed. His success followed many smart investments in real estate and he actually was the father of the shopping center concept. He owned countless shopping centers throughout Southern California. It just so happened that the Woodside Village Center we were looking at was his and he was concerned about its slow start until the area grew. He was trying to fill the empty space and make sure he obtained the right tenants. It showed even at his level he was interested in such a small detail as to check us out.

Obviously, Mr. E didn't have to work another day of his life, but in some way I think he enjoyed making the calls and his limited interactions with some of the day to day operation.

With Steve listening intently to every word he spoke; and going all out to please him, it was clear that Mr. E was his mentor and he was absorbing Mr. E like a sponge. He had more questions for us, and would take long pauses between answers as he digested our response. He shared a few more stories with us and before we knew it, the meeting was over. As we made our way down the elevator to the lobby, Steve said he could tell that Mr. E liked us. He never talks to anyone for that long. Let's see what he comes up with. A few days went by when we received a call from Steve. He wanted to come by and talk to us. The next morning he presented us with a manila folder marked *lease*. He said we passed the interview and Mr. Eichenbaum wanted us to take the space at Woodside Village. He was willing to take a chance on our idea. Steve said to look the lease over and he would answer any questions when he came by the next day. After Steve left, the reality set in that decision time was upon us. We were excited but nervous over the idea of saying our final yes. Could we do it? As we sat down that evening to look in the folder we were staring at a 3 inch thick stack of papers that were to be signed. There again, a little education on legal jargon would have been handy as we read through the pages.

We did understand the amount of the rent and length of the lease but not much more. Regardless, Steve came walking in bright and early the next day and after some small talk asked if we were going to go for it. Still not sure of ourselves, we surprisingly both said yes at the same time. Steve was visibly nervous by our instant answer. This was his first big assignment for Mr. E and he was real happy to close the deal. We spent the next fifteen minutes signing away. There was no turning back now.

Sometime later Steve did share with us that Mr. Eichenbaum had never had anyone point blank just sign a lease without dozens of changes. Of course, the lease was all certainly worded in their favor and Mr. E was just playing a hunch to see how well we would perform before he could throw the book at us. I guess our naiveté and inexperience was really showing, but in a way it worked in our favor. We were thrilled to just get our foot in the door and have the opportunity. We hoped it wasn't going to come back and haunt us down the road.

Steve Soberoff went on to become highly successful in real estate development in Los Angeles. He even ran for mayor of the city and became the Los Angeles Police Commissioner.

CHAPTER 15

MEAT MARKET FOR SALE

If we wanted to pursue our new dream of being delicatessen operators, we needed to do something in a hurry about getting rid of our current location. Our little meat market was our baby that we had struggled and nurtured to the point where it had finally provided for us. Obviously, we had mixed feelings. It had been quite a learning curve and we were attached to the little security it provided.

Selling a business was a whole new experience for us and we were clueless as to how to go about it. The big obstacle was to not only find someone who wanted their own business but they had to be a meat cutter. Now how many potential buyers could there be? When in doubt, don't do the obvious thing and call a business real estate broker. Instead, call the Penny Shopper and run an ad. Hey, it worked selling abalone...so why not a business?

After a few weeks we began to realize it was a lot easier selling abalone through the Penny Shopper. There were a few calls but no one had actually come to look. Early one morning, while I was grinding hamburger, I answered a call from a gruff sounding guy by the name of Sam Malone. He said he was a butcher in LA and had been looking for his own place. He wanted to come by the next day to check us out. I was all ears and I could not wait to tell Benny. We knew with the signing of the West Covina lease that time was running out and this might be our best shot at a sale.

The next morning we made sure we had everything cleaned, loaded and ready for meeting with Sam and the big show. The only problem was, it was in the middle of summer when a lot of our regular customers were away on vacation, the courthouse downtown was closed that week. It provided a lot of our lunch sandwich business and we were concerned we would scare him off if the business was not hopping.

As the meeting time grew closer and closer and not too many customers were in sight the bright idea was hatched to create a rush. We called Ben's wife and asked her to start dialing the store phone and we would pretend it was phone orders. We turned the ringer on the phone nice and loud so it would be heard. We stepped next door to our friends that ran the hair salon, Maxine and Sharon, Bobbi and Peter. We told them they were doing a story on our business and asked if they would help make us look busy by pretending to be customers and come in and place some orders when we gave them the signal.

Sam was a big, burly European guy...reminded me of Bluto, the strong man from the Popeye cartoons. He certainly wouldn't have any trouble wrestling around a side of beef. With his vice grip handshake I thought he was going to break my hand as he shook it. Not the kind of guy to mess with. Ben and I started showing him around…still a little early and not a customer in sight.

I was getting nervous, so I gave Ben the signal to call Lia for her round of phantom phone in orders to go. Jerry, one of the twins was working that morning to show that we even had an employee. Maybe that could make us appear even more credible. It was time to give Peter a call next door to send in the mystery shoppers. The phone started ringing off the hook as Benny was shouting out the details of the *to go* order. He no sooner hung up when the phone rang again with yet another order.

Sharon walked in and began ordering meat from the counter. Shortly thereafter, Maxine came in to place even more orders. Then Bobbi and Peter came in and Peter started telling Benny how much he enjoyed the steak from the night before. The acting was superb! We left Sam standing in the customer area to observe the wonders of his potential business while we handled the onslaught. It may have gone too far when Ben answered yet another call from Lia and shouted out an order for fourteen sandwiches. I sneaked a quick word with Ben and asked him to cut it out because we could hardly keep up. We have to make this believable! I know he was just messing with me because of the ridiculous scene that we had created. As luck did have it we had some regular business on top of the scene and we could see that *Bluto* was all eyes as he intently watched. Things did finally slow down enough for us to finish our pitch to Sam and as we walked him out the door we could only hope the performance would get an Oscar. We were on pins and needles for a few days until the vote was in. Big Sam finally came by to talk to us one evening after we closed. He made us an offer. I don't really recall the price…all I know is we took it and when he left we were jumping around like we had just won an Academy Award.

Mr. Eichenbaum had given us a few months to set up our new venture at his Woodside Village. We took a drive into Los Angeles looking for fixtures to outfit the place. We needed display cases, shelving, ovens, amongst all the other things we had no idea we needed since this was uncharted territory for us. After all, the meat shop we had was already set up when we took it over. We did have a business card for a Victor Refrigeration in Los Angeles. It had been given to us by Ingrid, the German lady at the restaurant where we ate breakfast most mornings.

We were driving through the industrial area near downtown over the classic 6th street bridge with the concrete river flowing beneath. Finally we pulled up to an old warehouse in the shadows of the tall buildings in Los Angeles. We slowly walked inside of the dimly lit wooden building. It felt like we were in a valley surrounded by stacks of old dusty display cases, used cash registers, shelving and ovens. This was the boneyard of past businesses that had seen their fifteen minutes of fame or just threw in the towel. Victor Refrigeration would sweep in, make an offer for pennies on the dollar then bring the truckload of failure down to the warehouse to refurbish and recycle to the next venture. We were next in line. We made our way to the windowless office area in the back to search out our destiny. The walls were lined with what seemed like hundreds of catalogs, manuals and trade books. A handsome wavy haired James Dean look-a-like quickly jumped up from his chair to introduce himself, "I'm Victor Cohen," he said confidently as we shook hands. A quite older gentleman sat over in the corner hallway slumped in his chair. He was planted in a large, comfortable wooden chair with a thick cushion. Hanging from his side was a large round ring of keys; I mean keys of every size, shape and alloy.

It appeared the old gentleman was actually Victor's dad. Maybe the Sr. Victor was just biding his time until young Victor could fly on his own, or more likely, just enjoyed coming down to the office to get out of the house. Probably sitting down along the ocean in Santa Monica wasn't his thing. Regardless, Young Victor was just as sharp and dynamic as he could be as he explained how they did business. When it came time to talk about how we were going to pay for things our ears perked up when Victor said he could possible outfit our store. We could give him a little down payment and were to make payments to him until paid in full. Of course there was this thing called *interest* involved. This was sounding like just what we needed since we had no clue as to what it would cost or for that matter, where to get the money.

Just across the room sat a sixty something year old guy at a draftsman table loaded with sharp pencils, rulers, templates and a long narrow light beaming on the desk. He was scrawling away on a plan laid out before him. Cigarette hanging from his mouth with maybe an inch of ash ready to fall and a stained coffee cup at his side. His name was Jack Koval. Jack asked what brought us boys downtown. As we explained our idea for the delicatessen, Jack nodded and took some notes.

Unfortunately, we did not have the sophistication to bring a blueprint of our space much less accurate dimensions. Jack agreed to take a drive out to West Covina the following morning to see what we had. True to his word he maneuvers into the parking lot in his big older model black Cadillac the next morning, the ever present cigarette hanging from his lip. He walks in and started measuring the space and making calculations and chalk marks on the floor. It became real apparent that even though Jack was not the owner of Victor Refrigeration he was the mastermind that had the savvy to put the pieces of the puzzle together. He was eying up the space and envisioning their used equipment inventory as to what would work for our project. We just stood there nodding. There was a lot more to this than we had envisioned. There were city plans, work permits, plan approval, health permits, spec sheets…a whole maze of rules and regulations to navigate. Jack had done hundreds of projects and knew exactly what we had in mind.

The following week we went back to LA and sat with Jack as he slowly uncoiled a fat roll of architectural plans. Across the top and perfectly hand printed in two inch letters it read…OLD WORLD DELICATESSEN / WEST COVINA. Everything was hand drawn to precision with every inch of the space accounted for as Jack rattled off rhyme and reason as to why he did this…and that. The code for this…the plumbing/electrical needed for that…on and on. I could feel he dared us to find an error which we wouldn't have recognized if there were one. He was a real artist at his trade! We did not have much to say except to shake our heads in agreement. We were in awe at how he put the puzzle together. It was a stroke of luck that we found Jack, and let's not forget Victor and his easy pay plan. Finishing up our business in Downey and letting go of the security and emotional connection of the first venture was falling into place.

Another bright spot was that the Meador twins wanted to work for us in our new venture in West Covina. Being devout Mormons they were waiting for their mission assignment and were willing to help us in the meantime.

CHAPTER 16

PIZZA

The Delicatessen we had in mind was patterned after New York Style Deli's. The display cases loaded with cheeses, corned beef, pastrami, breads, exotic meats, salads, and spreads. While we had a lot of mostly sandwich offerings for lunch, we needed to come up with something to offer at dinner. With Ben's Italian heritage the word pizza quickly came to mind.

The only catch was that we had zero restaurant experience and even though making a pizza at home could be done, how does it happen in a real pizza kitchen? Ben and I had several conversations about how we could learn that art. Turns out that Ben had a cousin who had a friend who was originally from New York who had moved to California and owned a small liquor store over in Montclair. He ran a pizza operation out of the backroom. With no address in hand, we decide to drive around the town of Montclair looking for a liquor store where you could buy a fresh baked New York style pizza.

We pulled up to a liquor store, ran inside, asked if they had pizza, waited for the guy at the counter to look at us like we were crazy, then ran back to the car and went to the next one. About the fifth or sixth stop a short skinny guy named Tony said sure we have pizza. The conversation immediately turned to New York and Benny's cousin and all things Italian.

After a while, Ben finally asked Tony if he would show him some of the basics of pizza making and asked if he could work there for free. He explained our location was 30 miles from there and we would never compete against his location. After a whole lot of hesitation, whether it was the brotherhood of fellow New York Italians or whatever, Tony finally agreed. Consequently, that Friday night Ben showed up to learn the ins and outs of Tony's operation. He went for several weekends to help and learn. On his way home at night he would stop by my house in Pomona near Lincoln Park and deliver one of his creations. They were getting better and better.

As with any skill or trade, and especially in a kitchen, you might visualize how it's done but the little nuances, moves, techniques, touches, tools, and recipes are vitally important and to get a chance to learn hands on is very special. Once you have the knowledge it might seem quite simple but the teaching and confirmation of the correct technique is very important.

Thank you to Tony for divulging some of the tricks of the trade and for Ben being sharp enough to pick them up. Now, if only Ben could just teach the boy from Indiana.

Victor delivered two truckloads of fixtures and began to put the puzzle together. Everything had been reconditioned, recycled, freshly painted or re-chromed. Old hinges and glass were replaced. It all looked as good as new to us. As a matter of fact, the display cases and bottle coolers had a certain retro/art deco look that had style lines that gave personality to the place. Jack had created a new bright orange shelving unit that stretched the entire length behind the display cases. We could load specialty canned items, pasta's and wines.

This added color for sure. Benny and I could not have been more proud and excited. I had just turned 25 years old. My wildest California dream was coming true.

We loaded the display cases with wheels of cheese, salami, and exotic Italian cold cuts. We stocked the shelves and prepared the sauces, sliced meats, condiments, made salads, hung the menu's, wiped off the windows, made signs for each item, mounted the grand opening banner and put up balloons.

Even though I enjoyed making signs, I knew my limits. I had searched out a real sign maker in Pomona by the name of Stewart Signs. He made all the signs for the L A County Fairgrounds and his work was unreal…all done by hand. We had him paint several 4x6 size banners on bright fluorescent paper stock. We made 5 or 6 big wooden A frames to which we attached the banners. The banners said things like:

NOW OPEN…N.Y. DELI…TASTY SANDWICHES FRESH SLICED COLD CUTS…PIZZA!

I realized there were sign ordinances about putting signs up on the street, but we thought by the time we were caught we could plead ignorance and at least get people to see our new store, which was slightly hidden from clear street view.

On the morning of the opening I was lugging these signs up Azusa Avenue., putting them in place every 50 feet or so, all the while keeping an eye out to see if I was going to get busted by the city.

Out of the corner of my eye, I spot a long black limousine that appeared to be following me and slowly driving along the curb a few hundred yards up the street. I was nearly done so it was too late to stop. As the limo came up beside me, the back window slowly rolled down. To my amazement the head of none other than Mr. Joseph Eichenbaum popped out. What timing on my part. Is this for real? Blood rushed to my face and as I sheepishly blurted out, "good morning Mr. Eichenbaum". There was a long pause and to my surprise, a big smile came over his face. He said in an excited voice, "These signs are a great idea…Good luck today!" With that, the limo whisked away as I stood there in disbelief.

Meanwhile, back in the kitchen, we were prepping the kitchen items and making our first batch of pizza dough from scratch. Ben had his recipe. I dumped a bag of flour on the big wooden bakers table. It was a used table, maybe 4 inches thick, originally thicker, but with the years of use from previous bakers constantly rolling and kneading dough it had worn down a few inches. We had sanded and cleaned the wood and were thrilled to have this relic .Benny proceeded to mound the flour and patterned out a well in the middle. He then added his yeast mixture, which was now bubbling.

Meticulously he slowly mixed the water and flour until it was creating a dough ball. Not too fast or you could ruin it. Electric mixer…What's that? We didn't have money for the luxury of an electric mixer so the pizza dough was made by hand. What a workout. Something about that dough was magical and the flavor was outstanding. I might add that we made dough this way for the first year until we saved enough money to buy a used Hobart mixer. I recall the day we used the new mixer and how amazed we were as we watched the dough effortlessly being mixed.

We also learned how to prepare pasta and lasagna with the aid of Ben's mom…the recipe was quite different and delicious. To give a New York flair to the menu, we called the traditional Italian combo sandwich a Brooklyn Bridge and a smaller version a Torpedo. Ben remembered the delicious eggplant sandwiches from his youth. We put it on the menu too, and, lest I forget, the meatball sandwich! The room was full of the aroma of homemade meatballs baking in the oven.

We opened on a Thursday without any advertising by merely turning the sign around. We were just busy enough that it enabled us to get our feet on the ground and learn how to cook our new items. We were very excited and wanted to make sure everything was perfect as customers trickled in for the trial run. We had done it! We were open!

Woodside Village is right next to La Puente California. It is more of a working class community. We knew nothing about demographics and really didn't care; all we knew was that they were all potential customers. The second night was Friday and let me tell you come Friday when the average working people get off for the weekend there is no hesitancy to spend money for food. Before we knew it, around 6 o'clock we were real busy. We were under fire for several hours and finished the night tired, yet overjoyed with the business. There is no more beautiful feeling than to take the gamble, put your idea together, nurse it along, jump through the hoops, do all the hard work and have a lot of luck fall into place, then…maybe then…see it actually succeed? To say we were happy would be an understatement. We replayed the night's rush…had a few laughs…cleaned up the kitchen, turned out the lights and went home happy.

CHAPTER 17

PANCHO

It would be hard to spend your life in Southern California and not run across someone famous…perhaps a movie star or a sports figure. In Indiana, there aren't too many famous people except, possibly a star high school or college basketball player one might bump into on a rare occasion. That was about as famous as it got where I came from.

So one day while working the counter at the West Covina Delicatessen, fate was about to deal me a hand. A lady…mid to late twenties, skinny, attractive and very bubbly…just an All-American girl came in. I recognized her as a regular customer who lived close by and was surprised when she knew my name. She introduced herself as Betty Stewart. She asked if I had a few minutes to talk. "Sure," I said." "Let's sit down."

Betty was there to ask me for a favor. She began by telling

me she had been a dental hygienist met this wonderful man who she just married. She wanted my help to impress him. I wondered where the conversation was going. The story continued that the family was going to have a big get together that weekend and she was going to order all the food and arrange all the details and she wanted my help to impress her husband that she was quite capable of handling everything. She went on to explain that she had not met much of the family; it was sort of a coming out affair for everyone to meet one another.

She planned to tell her new husband that she had gone to school with me and I was a good friend and willing to help. She asked if I could figure out the food they needed for the weekend and she would buy whatever I said. Also, she wanted me to provide a buffet for that Friday night when all the guests arrived. For sure, I didn't know what to think, but I was always up for a new adventure. The only catch…all of this was going to take place in Malibu…Malibu Canyon to be specific.

Without being pretentious, she told me her husband was Pancho Gonzalez, the tennis player. Coming from Indiana, if she had said Pancho Gonzalez, the basketball player I might have been much more impressed. Without hesitation, and with no thought as to how I was going to accomplish this, I said I would do it. I took the information and got directions to Malibu.

I told Ben about the meeting. Ben being older and always skeptical of my schemes looked at me like I was nuts. Do you know how far that is? Are you sure we can do that? Will we get paid? You went to school with her? As usual, he finally agreed to it. So I went about making a list. I tried to figure out what these people would eat in a weekend. They couldn't eat Deli food day and night.

My next door neighbor in San Dimas, Alfonso Reyes was a tennis fan. He was Mexican and had worked at Bank of America for some time in an upper level position in finance. How I knew he had a pretty good position was because I had incidentally asked him how to get a credit card and he brought me one the next day. On Saturday mornings when I was leaving early for work, he had his tennis racket in hand, headed for the courts.

He was wiry, maybe 5'2 wore glasses, and very smart. We joked around a lot and even erected a fence together between our new houses. I stopped by Alfie's house to see if he knew anything about Pancho? His mouth fell open when I told him I was going out to his place in Malibu to cater his family get together. He said Pancho had been No 1 in the world for nearly a decade and just recently had beaten 19-year- old Jimmie Conners in a tennis tournament despite being 44 years old. He said he was a fast living guy who drank cokes as he played, smoked cigarettes and didn't care who got in his way. He had a very fiery temper.

I began wondering if maybe I was in over my head this time. Alfie said Pancho had been married several times and had 6 or 8 kids…a big family! One thing I quickly understood was that Alfie adored Pancho.

Trying to figure out what to feed this clan was beginning to worry me. I consulted with Alfie and his wife, Bernadette, who I called Bernie, to get their input for some ideas about what to serve. I showed them the list of suggested food items

I had put together.

"Where's the Mexican food?" they asked

Laughing, I said to Bernie, "Fix them some of your tamales," which were the best I had ever eaten.

To my amazement she said sure. It suddenly made sense to have Mexican food for the event. "How about some enchiladas...rice and beans. How about those little round disk things that you make?" I was feeling a little bit better about the possibilities.

Before I knew it Thursday rolled around., Murphy's law started kicking in. We had a lot of business at the deli that Friday and were shorthanded. It would be impossible for Ben to come and help me in Malibu.

As a matter of fact ...no one was available to help me. Desperate for help, I called my trusty friend Mike Egan, the Irishman, who by that time was my kid's godfather. Mike had worked for years as a roofer. Solid built, he was strong as a horse. Mike was retired on disability and loved to pass the time stopping by the deli to do an occasional repair or at least make suggestions in his heavy accent that drove Bennie mad. He spoke that heavy Irish brogue that very few people could understand. Through intense concentration when he spoke, I learned to understand every word.

Christ Mac...he always called me Mac. I guess short for Romack...do you know what you're doing. He enjoyed good natured kidding. Yeah I will go. I stopped by Alfie and Bernie's on my way home .I was praying she hadn't changed her mind about preparing the Mexican dishes. Alfie had just arrived home from work. He said he was off Friday and would bring the food down to the Deli. A light went off in my head…Hmmm. I'm short of help…he is off…Mexican… loves Pancho! I blurt out "Why don't you come down to Malibu with me and give me a hand?" Well, he went blank for a minute…nervously he cracked a smile and agreed. As I left, I said "Be sure to bring your tennis racket".

Friday arrived. We had acquired an old panel truck that we used to go to LA to buy our daily produce. I got there early and scrubbed it out. I took my checklist out and started putting items in the truck. The Irishman arrived…Bennie rolled his eyes in the back of his head but managed to thank him for helping out. Finally, Alfie came walking in. I remember being relieved he wasn't wearing his all-out tennis wear. We took the trays of Mexican food, loaded them in the van and were finally on our way.

What a team I had assembled; Alfie, the Mexican in the middle and big Mike, the Irishman riding shotgun. What a threesome! Alfie didn't understand a word that Mike said all the way down there. But actually Mike's directions to Malibu were helpful. He said he had done a roofing job there a few years back.

I don't know if it crossed my mind that neither one of these guys had one minute of restaurant experience. We finally found Kannan Dume Road and started to wind our way into Malibu Canyon. After twisting and turning the curves and the load of food sliding all around, Mike shouted out a few *Christ Mac, slow down* outbursts as we searched for the address. It was not a house as I expected. It was a ranch…a tennis ranch. It was quite large, secluded and nestled in the hills. What a place!

Numerous tennis courts lined one side and a couple wings of apartments and cottages were near a main courtyard area. Perched directly above on a hillside was a beautiful home that was Pancho's house. A pink stucco main building looked to be the most obvious place for us to set up. Inside were a beautiful Spanish style dining/rec room with a stone fireplace at one end and a tremendous bar! We managed to find the kitchen and pulled the truck around to the entrance to unload.

I turned around and was met by a tall, tan, muscular figure with wavy hair. "Hello, you must be Randy," he said as he extended his hand.

He was the man...Pancho Gonzales. I introduced Mike and Alfonso. Alfie was star struck as he blurted something out to Pancho in Spanish. I tried to break the ice by saying Alfie was a big fan and loved to play tennis. That seemed to please Pancho and he laughed and said they would have to play. I have never seen a house that had a commercial kitchen and a large walk in refrigerator. I checked out the equipment as we unloaded.

Just as I thought things are going quite well, Pancho walked over to me and said, "So tell me Randy, what was Betty like in high school?"

I'm sure my face turned red as I tried to keep my composure. Well, here it goes I thought...hoped I didn't piss Pancho off...she was great...lot of fun. I remember the art class...Betty was good in art...and Mr. Maddock in history...Blah, blah, blah... and the dances were fun, too. Sure enjoyed being in high school with Betty."

I was thinking where do I stop and how can I get out of the

conversation? Pancho stood there sort of staring at me and finally said "I didn't know she was good in art.". Thank God, someone interrupted Pancho with a question and he left to take care of their request.

Just then, Betty...beautifully decked out...bubbly, perky and friendly came in to show me around and thanked me several times. She introduced me as her friend from high school. I stopped her as she began to walk away and said, "By the way I told Pancho, if he asks, that you were good in high school art." She laughed.

It was a few hours until we had to serve the buffet. Alfie even got a few tennis swings in with Pancho. Guests started arriving in droves. This was a big family! Aunts, uncles, sisters, brothers, cousins and friends of cousins! I found out that the Mexican people showed up when they were invited and when Pancho spoke...every one listened! The popular corner of the dining room quickly became the bar. Since they had no one assigned to the bar I asked the Irishman to help out. I remember Mike mixing me drinks at his kitchen sink so why not here.

Mike really took to it. He picked up Margarita making real fast thanks to Pancho's rather rotund sister giving instructions. Mike was the center of questioning about his accent and where he was from. He said he was from Argentina and then Israel. He was having a good time pouring tequila and trying to keep up with Pancho's family who were getting wilder by the minute. It was a stroke of luck that I brought Bernie's delicious food, for it was a big hit! Along with all the deli platters and salads, the buffet went great! Alfie was a natural helping with the food. His Spanish was also a big plus as he mingled with the guests.

With a family this large there were bound to be some who didn't get along with each other. I could see and feel the tension building between some of them. No matter how nice Betty was, Pancho's kids and sisters or whoever, did not seem to accept her with open arms. As the evening progressed and as Pancho sat at the bar sipping more and more tequila I noticed him looking around with a frown on his face. The scene was growing louder and louder.

The Spanish music was blaring in the background, when suddenly Betty came over to Pancho with tears in her yes. A few seconds later Pancho lunged across the room and with the speed he exhibited chasing a tennis volley, grabbed a guy and threw him against the wall. *GAME ON!* Bodies and bottles were flying, music played on, people screaming, both in English and Spanish…I even heard a little Irish thrown in. I thought "These Mexicans sure do know how to throw a party".

Fortunately we had already loaded up the truck. I waded through the mass of people to rescue the Irishman at the bar. I grabbed Alfie by the shirt collar as we zoomed by him and ran out a side door. We slammed the truck doors and weaved our way down Malibu Canyon to safety. Alfie sat shaking in the middle and the Irishman laughed and shouted one final…*CHRIST MAC!*

CHAPTER 18

A BIG BURDEN

There is no bigger burden than a great opportunity. Ambition is good, but it also has a terrible downside. There is often a struggle with balancing ambition with one's personal life. When a family is involved, time with them is often challenged by the need to spend time at the business. I believe most people have this dilemma, but perhaps an entrepreneur fights it more. I always tried to block out my addiction to ambition by making time for my family and really blocking out thought about the business from my head. Most of the time it worked!

Back in Indiana when I was growing up, my parents always took us for a Sunday drive. I have wonderful memories of driving to an Indiana State park or even just a shorter drive around the fringes of Indianapolis in the family Chevy. My dad was strictly a Chevrolet man. My sister

Nancy and I would pester him to a stop at Wilson's ice cream parlor for one of their famous thick malts. We always won!

Fast forward...I was some 2000 miles from Indiana doing the same thing with my family. We were out for a Sunday drive in the old Plymouth station wagon. Might sound trivial, but it felt good! One of my favorite drives was down Foothill Blvd, old Rt. 66. I snaked my way through Upland into the dense lemon and orange tree orchards. The beautiful river rock walls lined the road in many stretches.

We passed the old Sycamore Inn on the left and into Cucamonga and the grape vineyards...mile after mile of wineries and the vineyards all standing tall in perfectly aligned rows. Actually I learned that the Cucamonga area grapes dated back to the early 1800s and at one time over 20,000 acres were planted and supported as many as fifty wineries.

Often times we brought a picnic lunch to stop and enjoy as we took in the vineyards and the majestic snow-capped mountain peaks in the background. I never get tired of the mountain views in California. On the return drive it was interesting to see the little motels which dotted the old highway. They had seen their day; business dreams achieved...maybe dreams lost. I always imagined how it must have been when this road was the gateway to Southern California with old cars rambling along carrying folks to their own California dream.

This particular Sunday as I came down Foothill Blvd., near the eastern edge of Upland I noticed a storefront in a shopping center that was closed down. Dusty windows boarded up...obviously out of business. It had been a pie shop of all things. Feeling guilty that I even looked, after all this was family time, I could feel the twinge of ambition creep in...the light illuminating in my head and the, *what if?* question pulling at me. It was starting to get dark and I steered the car past the temptation.

Not able to free my mind of the potential of the location that I had seen the day before, I drove to Upland the next morning. I found the phone number for the owner of the shopping center from a neighboring merchant. Fortunately, the owner agreed to meet me later in the day.

He had just taken possession of the premises and asked what I had in mind. With our success in West Covina I felt a little more confident as I told him of the Old World Delicatessen and our desire to open at his location. He seemed interested and said he would call me the next day.

I could hardly wait to get back to West Covina to tell Benny. Benny was standing in front of a big pot of marinara sauce slowly stirring it as I spilled the news. Feeling a little surer of myself than when I talked him into selling the meat market he still kept his poker face and finally agreed to take a look at it.

The next day Ben and I met with Mr. Chandler to look at the space. The conversation went well and he appeared interested in our concept. The pie shop had spent a lot of money on a beautiful plank floor and dropped ceiling with ornate chandeliers. I remember thinking chandeliers...Mr. Chandler as I was trying to remember his name by making an association. The kitchen was in place and included a walk-in refrigerated cooler. Terms of the lease were discussed.

Chandler said he would throw everything in at no charge, even the chandeliers.

Benny and I were excited about this opportunity and really didn't give any thought as to how we would run a second location. We had a deal! We called Victor at Victor Refrigeration to see if Jack could make a run in his Caddy to check the store out. Jack, his usual confident, dry self, cigarette, dangling from his mouth, again measured, paused, thought for a while like the great *Carnac the Magnificent* until it came into focus. More than likely, Jack was thinking of what fixtures, lying in the back of the old warehouse, he could clean, sand, paint, and re-chrome to work the puzzle one more time.

Victor agreed to carry the loan since we had a good track record of paying him timely. Meanwhile Ben and I got busy cleaning, planning and figuring what style of deli we wanted. I recall being surprised as Bennie walked in with a load of lumber one morning; and in a matter of hours had made four nice displays that fit perfectly in the customer area.

The Old World Delicatessen in West Covina was mostly Italian style, but I felt that in Upland we could keep the Italian, and also bring in other ethnic taste. Benny agreed. Naturally, Jewish and deli go hand in hand. I made some trips into Los Angeles and found the Three Star Fish Company where I purchased beautiful lox to slice and. Lake Superior smoked white fish; even a barrel of pickled herring.

I was busy figuring out recipes for liver pate, double whipped cream cheese, chicken and tuna salads. Greek and German products were searched out as well. I was having fun, but actually wondered if we could really sell this stuff.

That barrel of pickled herring might have been too much. Upland was a more affluent community and I hoped they would like what we were going to offer.

Finally, the big day arrived. Jack had come through once again. The display cases were fantastic! The clean modern lines looked sharp with the beautiful plank floor. The chandeliers gave the place a touch of class. We even had a refrigerated pastry case. We had that adrenaline rush of excitement and yet were scared to death. We had spent every penny we could get our hands on…this better work!

We decided I would stay in Upland and Ben would make sure the original store in West Covina ran smoothly. There were few employees to spare in West Covina for the new store. I hired a couple people that just happen to come in looking for a job. Ben's retired father-in-law, Joe Vitale, whom you may recall helped cater our first wedding, was even called into service.

He busied himself cracking the green Italian olives with a wooden mallet, and then marinating them with olive oil and spices. He surprised me by coming up with an Italian garden salad that had a variety of fresh chopped vegetables in a tasty dressing. I latched onto any available family member or acquaintance.

That Friday morning the big day had arrived…Sal from Villa Rosa bakery in San Gabriel delivered fresh Italian breads and rolls along with trays of Italian pastries: cannoli's, napoleon, éclairs, rum-ba-ba's, and a variety of fruit tarts. I made a connection in LA with Old Country Bakery and they had a truck deliver gorgeous, Kaiser rolls, onion rolls, sheepherder bread, Jewish egg bread and bagels.

We had fresh bread stacked everywhere. We went so far as to get fresh Greek baklava pastry from a baker in Long Beach.

So we turned the **OPEN** sign around and within an hour it was off to the races! It became a *feeding frenzy* as we struggled to keep up. We were busy slicing meats, and cheeses. The lox was popular and it was difficult to slice paper thin as requested. Dipping up salads, making sandwiches, all the time moving from one end of the counter to the other doing my best to assist inexperienced workers and praying no one would get cut. This was the first time many had touched a non-forgiving meat slicer.

Since our store was in the center of the shopping center we had a lot of shoppers walk by our front windows. We had found a rather large hot dog display that slowly baked the hot dogs as they rolled around. It too was an instant hit. I believe we were selling the dogs 2 for $1.00 at the time. We used top quality kosher hot dogs we picked up in Los Angeles from a kosher meat company.

Ben had remembered his favorite hot dog stand in New York which sautéed fresh onions in a marinara sauce to offer as a topping .They were absolutely delicious!

It took one employee to man the hot dog station. The grilled skirt steak sandwich along with the meatball sandwiches were flying out the door.

As the day played out, and with everyone exhausted, I turned the CLOSED sign around. While I surveyed the damage, the meat case display was in total disarray; the salads were gone, the pastries were…wiped out and one lonely loaf of bread remained on the counter. All the doubts about the location…the concerns about paying the debt…the questions of could we make it…were all answered by the battle that had just ended. We were obviously elated and on our way.

After I came down from the high of the first day again the reality of being open every day and the logistics of running this operation began to set in. Being young and running on adrenaline and at that time unlimited energy, I eagerly jumped out of bed and headed to work each morning.

As anyone in business will tell you the biggest challenge is the employees. We had hired four or five employees at our first deli in West Covina, although Ben and I did most of the work. Now I needed at least twelve to handle the new place and I needed them now! I drove over to Upland high school and spoke to their work experience teacher to help recruit. I ran an ad in the old standby Penny Saver newspaper. I was fortunate to hire Henry Altman, a retired Jewish deli operator from New York. It was as if I called central casting in the movie industry and said send me an actor who looks like he runs a New York deli. His son was, get this, a prominent gynecologist in town. Henry was a character, a real New York accent and full of personality.

The younger workers annoyed him at times. He loved working the counter just for something to do. Henry gave the place some charm and made us look a little more credible, especially since I looked more like a teenager than an *old world* deli operator. With a little luck we filled the gaps until we had a decent crew trained and running.

The store was hopping all the time and it was especially hectic on Saturdays. We had bread stacked across the display cases several feet high and I could tell if we were having a good day when, as we sold the breads, we could finally see the customer face to face. I can still smell it to this day !What a wonderful atmosphere the fresh breads created.

With Cucamonga just down the road and, come to find out, a nice Italian community, the place became a favorite with them since we offered all their favorite deli items; prosciutto, copocolla, mortadella, pecorino romano off the wheel, various salami's. I came to realize many of these people were the families who owned and operated the wineries that I often went by on my Sunday drives. We also offered some Italian grocery items. Wine was a natural to stock in our operation and we were interested in offering unique local wines.

Seems like it was right on cue, for while I was waiting on an older Italian gentleman who looked like the *Godfather,* I struck up a conversation. He proceeded to tell me he, indeed was a wine maker, He introduced himself as Dom. We became friendly and he offered to bring a bottle of his wine for us to try. Who was I to argue with the *Godfather.* In just a few hours he came back with several bottles. He said the vast majority of his wine was already sold and went to New York. Being raised in a very conservative home that didn't allow alcohol, I knew zero about wine.

Ben, on the other hand enjoyed wine with nearly every meal. He was surprised when I gave him the bottles. He even showed them to his neighbor who was a wine lover and told Ben how this particular vintage was highly sought after.

To my surprise, a few days later another older Italian gentleman was buying cheese from me and come to find out, he too made wine. Of course I told him that I had spoken to Dom, another winemaker and he had given me bottles of his wine. He had a surprised look as he introduced himself as Vito. His wife spoke up and said Vito and Dom were brothers. She said she would bring me some of their wines. She returned shortly with even more bottles than Dom had given me. "Try these, you will like them."

I put the wines on the counter and started waiting on another customer. The next customer, who had been standing there as I took the wines laughed a little and told me how the two winemaking families were very well know and the two brothers had split up in a family feud. Each now had their own winery and had not spoken to each other in years.

As things progressed, and Dom found out Vito had also been there with his wine and offered to sell it in the delicatessen you could feel the jealousy in his voice. To disarm the situation I said, "Dom I know you don't sell your wine in California and I didn't want to ask you to sell it here." He finished buying his cold cuts, pasta and left.

Within an hour he had a younger man wheel in five or six cases of wine. Dom walks in with a determined smile on his face and says in his broken accent, "Now…you will sell the very best wine". As I stood there dumfounded I paused…then started looking around to see if his brother Vito was coincidentally walking in to get his weekly fix of Pecorino Romano. Luckily…he was nowhere in sight.

CHAPTER 19

REALLY IN A PICKLE

When you think delicatessen, you think pickle, right? Well, at least I do. I was in search of the best pickle in California and I found it in East Los Angeles of all places. A-1 Eastern Pickle sits in a semi residential/commercial area behind the General Hospital. The building, or actually warehouse, was an old winery many years ago. It's quite a building with brick walls three feet thick…no earthquake will take it down. I think it is on Johnston Street, just off Main. Maury and Murray bought the property, way back when. They not only had this magnificent building, but owned dozens of small bungalows up and down Johnston street and the street behind the warehouse. All these houses were rented to the employees. Talk about a pickle kingdom. It reminded me of playing Monopoly and the little green houses you bought as you accumulated more money. Years ago they started picking up cucumbers at the LA produce market and pickled them with their spice concoctions.

One thing led to another...The walls were soon stacked twenty feet high with barrels of pickles as the word spread. They would age for a few months and then transform them into the most delicious pickle you ever bit into. They had that snap, and the hint of garlic that defines a properly put together pickle. They also made the greatest sauerkraut, yellow hot peppers, Greek peppers and even pickled green tomatoes.

I was immediately hooked on these pickles. Maury or Murray...I never was able to match the right one with the right name. I usually guessed wrong. We hit it off pretty well and they allowed me stop by his pickle factory and buy direct.

The pickles were a big hit in the delicatessens and I went so far as to drive from my Romack's Delicatessen in Lake Arrowhead and load my old Dodge truck with barrels of pickles. Each barrel contained a couple hundred pickles. I bought 10 or 12 barrels, along with a few barrels of the sauerkraut that I used in our Reuben sandwiches.

One such trip, I will never forget. I went into LA early one morning to pick up some produce and noticed I had room for some pickles I could squeeze into the very rear of the Dodge cargo space. I had one of those shells that covered the bed of the truck so you could actually put a lot of merchandise in the back. I went by A1 Pickle and bought ten barrels. Maury, or was it Murray jumped onto a fork lift and brought the barrels out for me to load. I manage to squeeze them into the limited space I had saved. I shut the tailgate and closed the door of the shell cover and off I went.

I drove down the 10 freeway the forty miles or so to San Bernardino and decided to stop and buy gas before starting up to Lake Arrowhead. I pulled up to the pump, got out and walked to the rear of the truck. You should have seen my face when I saw that the tailgate of the truck had dropped down and was open. I immediately looked in the cargo area.

I was horrified when a quick count revealed not ten, but six barrels sitting there. Big Problem! Somewhere between Los Angeles and San Bernardino the rear tailgate fell open and four barrels of kosher pickles had flown out onto the freeway. The tops of the barrels did not have lids, but just a rubber band securing the plastic liners. Can you picture that? Every mile or so a barrel, with a couple hundred pickles exploding onto the highway. I didn't know what to do…the damage was already done.

I quickly turned on my radio to see if a Sig Alert had been called on the 10 freeway for flying pickles scattered on the freeway. None had and I sheepishly drove home waiting for the call where the police had tracked down that nut that dumped hundreds of pickles on the San Bernardino freeway. I gave a big sigh of relief when no calls came.

Pickle problems have a way of haunting me. Ben and I had scraped up enough money in West Covina to take the empty space next door and add seating for our customers. Ben bought some heavy timber and made twelve or more picnic tables that we stained. They actually looked pretty sharp. We decorated the room quite nicely and were really proud of it. I had the bright idea of placing a giant barrel of pickles at the end of the counter It was serve yourself…sort of a novelty. The customers could pick their own pickle right out of the barrel, put it in a bag and then pay at the counter.

We had just had the new addition open a few days. Ben and I were proudly standing over to the deli side of the restaurant and admiring our work. We had several tables of families dining. They were enjoying the pizzas and sandwiches. Off to the side and at a corner table I happened to catch a lady discreetly changing a baby's diaper. To my horror, when she finished she started walking around the room looking for the trash can to dispose the diaper. You guessed it. That barrel of some 300 pickles, were mistaken for a trash can!

She raised the hinged cover as I lunged across the room trying to stop her. It was too late! The soiled diaper was put into my big barrel of pickles. As you would expect, she was apologetic, but what could I do? To make matters worse I grabbed a dolly and wrestled it under the barrel to get it out of there. Benny was using some choice words as he opened the backdoor to help me dump it all in the trash. If you ever messed with trying to maneuver a barrel around, especially one with several hundred pickles and a soiled diaper, it's pretty tricky. As I tried to roll the barrel out the back door I lost control...The barrel got away from me and fell on its side.

Picture this... the pickles and the diaper went streaming down the back alley like a flash flood. Ben and I stood there laughing. Hey, running a business is not always pretty!

CHAPTER 20

DAD, CAN I GO TO WORK WITH YOU?

Every kid becomes curious about what their dad does when he goes *to work*. I was no exception. My father worked in Indianapolis on the New York Central Railroad for over thirty years. His job was that of a switchman/yard conductor. He usually went to work in the evenings and worked well into the night. He would ride around the rails sitting in the caboose…the last, usually red car of a typical freight train.

The caboose was technically his rolling office and even had a desk. Indianapolis was an industrialized city with a lot of factories, and the rails were the way the factories distributed and received goods. Dad would have a list of the rail cars that needed to be taken from the factory and coupled onto the main rail to its final destination.

What kid is not fascinated by a train? I certainly was, and living just a hundred yards or so from the tracks as a kid was fun to hear the train whistles and see the iron beauties flying by. Now my dear mother might not have been that excited about living so close to the tracks. We never even considered that maybe we didn't live in the most desirable area of Indianapolis. We loved it there. The smoke from the constant train traffic would drift over to our house and I'm sure created a lot of work to keep the house clean. We regularly cleaned the wallpapered walls several times a year by rolling a clay type cleaning dough ball over the walls to pick up the film of accumulated soot. The kids found it fun! My mom… not so much.

Every afternoon near dusk, the South Wind passenger train would zip by on its way to Florida. It was fascinating to wonder, who the passengers were and what exotic places they were going. The beautiful stainless steel plated cars were loaded with passengers. We were close enough to see the faces of those seated on the train. The dress of the day was suits and ties for men. The women were dressed in their very best outfits, complete with hats and gloves. We especially looked for the dining car and watched people sitting at tables and being served by the Negro porters, all outfitted in starched white uniforms with round hats.

My sister Nancy and I would stop playing kickball when we heard the whistle far away and run closer to the tracks to wave as they whisked by. It made our day when they waved back. We never even gave danger a second thought. As a matter of fact, we could play out on the streets until the street lights came on automatically…then we hurried home before mom came looking for us.

I recall my dad's ritual getting ready for work. He wore

his bib overalls, a railroad hat, with a New York Central patch, a red scarf around his neck, and a big pair of heavy work boots. Thick gloves hung from his pocket. The final touch was his beloved lantern; always tuned, shined, and ready to go. It was operated with a dry cell battery and was his means of communicating with the engineer as they negotiated the maze of tracks picking up box car after box car to assemble a complete train. It was done strictly with light signals from my father's lantern as they passed through the long Indianapolis night.

My dad had no commute to work; he merely crossed the street and hopped on a train. I never gave a thought as to how odd that was. When my father would return from work in the middle of the night he would always give a familiar knock on the door with his big burley fingers in a fluttering motion against the glass. It was a duh...duh...duh ...duh... twice over. This was his signal before he entered. I still could recognize that knock to this day. As a kid, and laying there in bed; it would make you feel safe, and you felt secure in knowing dad was home.

In the winter months when Indiana was cold, I mean really cold, he would be so bundled up in long underwear, a couple of shirts, a heavy coat and a hat with ear flaps. The scarf covered most of his face. He had rosy red parched cheeks from the cold. I never really appreciated it till years later, as I got older, as to how terribly dangerous his work had been. I came to realize what a truly wonderful provider he was and the risks he endured to provide for the family. It must have been quite challenging to be out in the pitch dark, walking along the switching yards, constantly on the alert for obstacles to be avoided. He was required to jump on and off of moving trains as they passed by, which made it even more demanding. If that weren't enough, add in the factor of doing this in zero weather during the winter, often in ice and snow. I don't see how he did it for all those years without being seriously injured or killed.

Maybe his example instilled a little of his work ethic in me. One afternoon as my dad was leaving for work, I asked him, as I had several times, if I could go to work with him. I must have been every bit of 7or 8 years old. Maybe he had been concerned about taking me on prior occasion because of my fragile gangly look and knowing I would have to climb up on the trains. To my surprise, he said he would return for me in a few hours. It was a beautiful Indiana summer night. We made our way down the street past a few tracks and when I looked up, I saw a large locomotive spewing steam out all around it as it stood still waiting for my dad. Of course, it was highly illegal for me to be with him. His fellow railroad men were extremely nice to me. I heard them say they would keep an eye out for the *railroad Dick*. We walked along several freight cars attached to the locomotive until we came to the caboose. Dad hoisted me up on the big iron stairs and told me to go on in.

I entered the big sliding door and walked across the plank floor. I noticed the wooden desk where my dad worked. Benches lined the walls, and there was a potbellied stove at one end, which was obviously fired up on those cold winter days. Dad was quite a cook and made soups or a pot of beans for the crew. An ice chest/water cooler dispenser was beside the desk with a paper cup holder attached. The windows slid open for a wonderful breeze to cool the night. Midway down one side was a ladder. Out of curiosity, I climbed the ladder to a cozy cubicle that had windows all around with a view down the line. Cushioned seats lined the *eagle's nest*.

The train slowly started to roll. The sound of the rickety wood and fixtures shifting created a distinct melody as we picked up speed. Dad told me to stay inside while he did his work and if anyone came to go hide upstairs. He was gone twenty or thirty minutes at a time using his lantern to select boxcars around the city and coupling them to the train. As we rolled along the tracks between stops, I stood on the back porch area, blew the whistle that was attached to the railing and waved at the cars stopped at the crossings as we rumbled by.

Late into the night dad came back to the caboose and told me to follow him. We walked past several freight cars of the train we were forming and there in all its mighty glory stood the train's engine that had been pulling us all night. I felt like an ant standing next to an elephant. The steam was slowly clouding around the giant wheels. There was a slight hissing sound as it stood by waiting for the engineer to let it loose.

We climbed this behemoth and went through a door and all of a sudden, I was standing next to the engineer himself. He was perched up in a large leather seat surrounded by gauges, levers, pipes and mirrors. He was very friendly as he greeted me, but always keeping one eye out the open window and the other on the controls. He had me pull on a chain that blasted the air horn. It was quite a thrill for a kid! Dad let me sit on a large leather bench across from the engineer. He had to leave the engine to finish the assigned list. One thing that I remembered about the engine was the cool night air and how extremely warm it was in that control room compartment.

After midnight, I slumped over and immediately fell asleep. The next thing I remembered was being in my dad's arms as he climbed down off that iron horse with me. He carried me across several sets of tracks and into our house. The night's work was over. But the memory lives with me forever!

FAST FORWARD

What goes around…comes around. I now had a family and my kids would ask to go to work with me. Dawn is my oldest daughter and was the first who asked this question. I had my first business and she would come with me to help dad. Dealing with a child's attention span was the biggest challenge. I would let her sweep the floor and maybe help me clean the windows. We had just started making shish-k-bobs and assembling them was a tedious task. They had become quite popular and we needed a lot. So she would sit and thread the wooden sticks with the beef chunks, fruit, and vegetables. I made a deal to give her a dime for each one. After we would prepare a big pan, I would let her calculate how much I owed her. If her calculation was right she received an extra dollar. This occupied her for a while. Then I took her around the corner to the Meralta Theatre to see the latest Disney movie. Mr. Cummings was not only my landlord but he owned two theaters on Downey Ave. and admission was free and he always gave us a giant bag of popcorn. It made for a fun day!

A year or two later, my wife needed a break so I volunteered to take my two daughters to work with me. The younger daughter Dee Dee was probably five. She was starting to ask to go to work with dad so I thought this was the perfect opportunity. Dawn, her big sister, at nine, naturally wanted to come along, which was fine with me! At the time, I had the Upland Delicatessen. Therefore, I took the girls in and found some easy task for them to do. Sweeping the floor and cleaning windows worked for a while. I was dealing with their attention span and was aware that I better keep them occupied. I let them mess with my sign making kit. They made some pictures with the ink pens. Having a great time! Lunch time comes and, since their mom wasn't around I let them eat whatever they wanted: hot dog, soda, French fries, cream puff pastry…all that healthy stuff.

I had a meeting to go to just down the street. Maxine was an older lady who worked for me and just happened to be working that day. She was very responsible, so I asked if she could keep an eye on the girls until I returned from my meeting. I didn't think I'd be too long. She was happy to do it. I let the girls sit in the storage room. It had a table for them to color on or whatever. I told them they could assemble a few of the pink cardboard cake boxes. We sold lots of pastries and it was easy for the employees to grab a box that was already assembled and put the customer's selection in the box. It was a hassle to assemble the box in front of the customer. So I showed them how to do one. How you fold along the creases and bend it just right, then carefully insert the flaps one at a time. With their tiny hands they could hardly do it but seemed to enjoy trying. I figured this was good for fifteen or twenty minutes, then they could color some more.

Off I went to my meeting. The meeting dragged on a lot longer than I anticipated and when it was finally over I was concerned because I knew the girls would be really bored waiting for me that long. Finally I made it back to the deli. I always park in the back and entered the back door directly into the kitchen. As I open the back door, I noticed the lights were out…Hmmm...it was very quiet.

When I reach over and flicked the switch on, I heard two little voices scream, "Surprise Dad!" To my amazement, I was standing in a *pink tunnel*. Pink was everywhere. It actually was quite beautiful! There were pink cake boxes stacked from one end of the kitchen to the other and several feet high. They not only had assembled all these boxes but had made this maze to walk through. I was stunned!!! They had really pulled a joke on Dad. I stood there laughing with Dee Dee and Dawn .I realized they picked up the task of folding the cake boxes quite well…too well. Another wonderful moment to always remember!

CHAPTER 21

MOUNTAIN ESCAPE

Ben and I went on to open a third successful Delicatessen in Lavern, California. By this time and at the risk of sounding over confident, we were pretty self-assured with how to set up shop and make a go of it most anywhere. I started having additional thoughts creep into my mind.

I was having doubts about staying in Southern California. Even with the success, I wondered what it would be like to live in Indiana at a slower pace, maybe have some acreage, relax more, and enjoy old friends, family, and familiar places, in addition to being around my parents as they were retiring. I don't care where you're from, it could be the flatland of Nebraska or the hills of Tennessee; where you were born and raised is home. Anyone who has moved away will tell you that.

On the other hand, you are looking at it through rose colored glasses, and the real reasons you left are pushed to the back of your mind and you mostly remember the good. During this time of indecision, I went as far as to sell my interest in Old World to Ben and keep a distributing company we had formed. Ben and I are very close friends to this day. With what we had been through we have a wonderful bond that is special. We sure accomplished a lot together.

Within a few months of running the distributing company I started to get the itch to own a delicatessen once again. It was the customer interaction, the thrill of a rush that I really missed. I guess it was fate, but as luck would have it, I stumbled across a location on Foothill Blvd. in Glendora, California. The hurdle of getting a property owner to believe in me and give me a chance was a lot easier with my previous track record. I opened a delicatessen and named it Chicago Sausage Company.

Using the same format as before, I was fortunate that it worked and I had wonderful success from day one. I sold the distributing company and settled down to just running the deli and minding my own business. I had a comfortable home in Claremont, California.

I coached some Little League, traveled a little and should have been quite content. However, as any entrepreneur will tell you…I guess I qualify to call myself that since I have learned how to spell it, there is always an itch to try something new. To see what's behind that door. I'd like to do it one more time. The desire or calling, to start something new was still there. Although, I had definitely wanted to move somewhere with a slower pace, living in California was exciting! You get hooked! You get spoiled with the perfect weather. Not to mention, the plentiful selection, year round of fruits and vegetables. The scenery is spectacular! Ocean, desert, mountains…yet, there was something missing. Little did I know when I opened the deli in Glendora that it would provide a connection to the missing link.

To put it in a dramatic way, *an escape!* The representative of the owners of the center, and the guy I signed with, was Jerry Kittrell. Jerry and I were becoming pretty good friends. He would stop by the deli and have a beer, always Miller Lite. Jerry was the mirror image of a young Robert Redford and had the following of girlfriends to prove it. He was from Texas, and a big Texas longhorn fan, obviously a Texas grad. I enjoyed talking to him. During one of these conversations I shared with him the fact I was getting tired of the rat race in Southern California and was seriously considering moving back to Indiana. He certainly understood, with his obvious affection for all things Texas.

Within a week, Jerry stopped by with some news to share. His company George Coult Properties had just made a deal to redevelop a property that he thought I might find interesting. He said, "If you want to get away from it all I have the place for you!" It's called Lake Arrowhead. He explained it was in the San Bernardino Mountains. The village located on the lake had been there for many years and his company was going to redo the entire town. He said if I wanted to come aboard just let him know. He would give me first choice of a location within the complex. "Go check it out," he urged.

Just a few days later, I quietly took a drive to San Bernardino and looked for Waterman Avenue, which turned into Highway.18 on the approach to the foothills of the mountains. Being a *flatlander*, that first drive up the mountain to Lake Arrowhead was a thrill! The highway is called *Rim of the World* and it becomes real apparent how it obtained its name. The road is virtually carved out of the side of the mountain, and being only two lanes in most sections, you had better concentrate. Once I get over my queasiness, the views are spectacular. It is one of the most radical descents of a road in the world. The climb is 5,200 feet or a *mile high*. You weave down winding roads lined with massive pine trees into a valley and start to see blue water between the trees. When I finally came to a clearing, the view was breathtaking! I had arrived!

The lake was formed a hundred years ago to collect water that would irrigate the citrus groves in the valleys below. The results were stunning! Clear blue skies! Snow-capped mountains! Crystal clear water! Quite a sight! Clean air with the scent of pine! What's not to like?

The new village was just starting to take shape. Jerry had given me a plan of the new layout as to where each building was to be placed. Most every location had stunning views of the lake. It was going to be a difficult decision to even come up here on top of this mountain, much less what building to select? There was a question about where I'd find customers.

I had a lot of thinking to do. Jerry came by the delicatessen a few days later and wanted to know if I was interested. I had a flashback to being in the meat shop and the snap decision that was made to *go for it* with the first delicatessen lease.

Jerry had a waiting list of other potential restaurant operators and wanted to give me first crack, but he needed a fast decision. Now I know, I had a habit of making impulsive decisions just from *my gut feeling*...somehow...someway... it all works out! So why stop now as I blurted out the words, "Sure I'm in."

The logistics of making it all work, after I said yes, required not only selling my house and moving the family to the mountains, but finding a buyer for the Glendora delicatessen.

Unlike selling the meat market a few years ago, this business had a pretty good track record. The population in California had a lot of Asian influx. Peter Wang, a tall, skinny, neatly dressed South Korean with a big smile was full of questions. All the right questions! After showing him around and discussing figures he seemed interested. Unlike me, he was smart enough to think before he leaped.

But leap he did...and we had a deal. I agreed to train Peter and actually felt confident enough to carry a note on the business and let him make monthly payments. My decision to trust him worked out as time proved. He made every payment on time and even paid the note off early.

Skipping past the boring details...I was off to the mountains and Lake Arrowhead! At about the same time, my younger brother Bill was now living in California. He was available to work with me and wanted to join me in the mountains. Bill was seven years younger than I, free spirited and had great people skills. Actually, he had worked at the upscale, exclusive Columbia Club in Indianapolis as a waiter. He was friendly and outgoing. Bill would be a big asset, and besides it would be nice to be around my family again. Timing a move like that was difficult and we were still a few months from having the new venture ready.

SAVED BY THE ELVES

In the meantime, the village was nearly complete. Many of the shops were opening and the place was full of excitement and activity as the merchants were putting their final touches on their shops. Plans were made to have a big grand opening party. Jerry called and asked if we would cater the event. There would be around two thousand people in attendance. Yes, we were interested in the challenge, without giving it a thought as to how we could do such a big event. It was a chance for the new Romack's Arrowhead Delicatessen to show what it could do! This was definitely going to be pressure packed since we were on a lake… maybe *sink or swim* would be a good way to describe the possibility. Bill and I got busy trying to figure how to pull this one off. We did have one major obstacle to overcome… We had no kitchen! We scouted around the village site and figured where to put up a big tent to house the buffet we were planning. We decided on an unoccupied building near the tent could be our makeshift kitchen. We worked away on the menu. We rented equipment to prepare the food.

Our menu was going to be appetizers, finger food items such as grilled shrimp, skewers of threaded steak and chicken and stuffed mushrooms. I also went to an LA cheese distributor and purchased several dozen wheels of unique cheeses to display and serve. In addition, I had my Jewish baker bake giant loaves of egg twist breads, rye breads, sheepherder bread. These giant breads were quite a conversation piece and would enhance our display of cheese wheels. To go along with the food were two complete well stocked bars to serve drinks. We needed to find some bartenders. Since

Bill had worked around a bar at his club job in Indianapolis, he figured out the alcohol order. We bought several dozen cases of liquor, wine and mixer items to set up the bars. Bill was renting the upstairs of a house directly across the street from the village. As with a lot of mountain homes it had a very high pitched roof to keep snow from accumulating on top. His windows were where the gables were and the house sat quite high overlooking the lake. A quirky narrow catwalk led to his front door. These unusual designed older homes added to the charm of the village area. We stored the booze in Bill's front room until the big day. His place was built like a fortress and had a very thick front door with a strong lock, so there was no worry about security.

The day of our big debut had arrived. We began early in the morning. I had enlisted a few local people to help prepare the appetizer and grill items. We set up the tables, made a list, figured strategy and tried to not leave any stone unturned. Desperate for bartenders, I resorted to calling my old friend Mike, the Irishman, from Pancho Gonzales fame, to help us out. He also agreed to pass by Pasadena and pick up two large ice carvings I was having made for the center-pieces of the buffet. I guess we were going all out!

The clock was ticking…we seemed to have the food layout under control. The Irishman pulled up in his old Chevy pickup truck. He brought his niece, Lennie to give us a hand. I think he knew from past experience with me that I could grossly underestimate the task at hand. Lennie was a highly skilled surgical nurse, so I quickly figured she could carve and be in charge of the cheeses. How I came to that assumption, I don't know, but she went along with it. Mike also brought his next door neighbor, Linda, to help she could help put out appetizers.

Mike had the two large ice carvings in the back of his truck covered with tarps. He really liked the challenge and to my surprise, they had not even started to melt. Time was running out. We were getting closer to the start. Bill and I decided to jump in the truck and go get the alcohol at his house. When you're pressured and under fire…Murphy's Law seems to kick in. We pulled up in front of Bill's house and as we were running up to his door he announces with panic in his voice, "I don't have my key!"

To make matters worse he had no idea where it was nor what we could do? Breaking down the door was not an option and as we looked up at the dizzying height of the house, the open window high above in the gable would be impossible to reach. We were running out of time. As we were standing there Bill's next door neighbors were pulling in. The two brothers were real mountain characters. Small in stature, they always seemed to have a comical little grin on their face. The red beanie type stocking hats they always wore added to their character.

We always jokingly called them the two *elves*. Jack and Jake were tree cutters, and they were quite muscular and lean to the point they appeared walked sort of hunched over.

We quickly explained our dilemma as they stood there with

those grins on their faces. I pointed to the only way through the open window in the gable high on top of the house! They thought for a minute, and then went to work. They had large braided ropes in their truck they were throwing up on the roof. I had no idea what they were doing. They were scurrying around the roof...like...well...like trolls. Just a few minutes later Jake was being lowered, from the peak of the house, with a rope around his waist. He dangled into the open gable window as if it were a game. Bullseye! He then charged through the house to unlock the door. As he swung the front door open, Bill and I breathed a big sigh of relief.

The boys had saved the day! We were really cutting it short on time. Jack and Jake were getting a big kick out of it and volunteered to help. They said they would change clothes and come right over. We zoomed across the street with the cases of booze and quickly started stocking the bars. We were down to the last minutes. We had all the cheese and bread display setup; the chafing dishes were hot with the flames under them.

Beautiful flowers were lined along the buffet table. Lastly, we unloaded the two ice carvings and placed them in the center of the table. The first ice carving was a giant replica of the Lake Arrowhead Village logo and the second was a giant dolphin. The sculptors stood about four feet high and were a spectacular crown to top off the display. They were in great shape with just a slow drip from the dolphin's nose. This was proof that they were truly ice. The music started...guests started to arrive by the hundreds.

Bill and I were flying around restocking the buffet, grilling appetizers, talking to guests. We were in constant motion. Now the bar scene was interesting. We had big Mike, the Irishman mixing drinks together with his two elf helpers. Jake and Jack had dressed pretty sharp with rolled up white shirt sleeves and matching ties. Actually, as it turned out, the joke was on me, for they were quite experienced as bartenders and not only rescued the booze, but were real fast at dispensing it.

As the night finally wound down and I surveyed the situation, it was apparent we had a big crowd. It seemed like we had just been through a battle of sorts. Lenny and Linda were exhausted and had blisters on their hands from cutting cheese all night. There was just a small wedge left. Mike and the elf brothers had nearly gone through all the beverages. The food chafing dishes were empty. The giant ice sculptors were melting, with a more constant drip from that dolphin's nose. There were many wonderful comments and great reviews. We were tired, but it was a good tired.

We had made it! My brother Bill and I gave each other a big victory hug.

EPILOGUE

As I reflect upon my answer to that question from long ago of, "What do I want to be when you grow up"? I think I would still climb on that Schwinn Red Phantom and deliver that paper route. And when I walk by a beautiful meat display and recognize all the shapes, sizes and names of all the meats, I just know I could make those cuts as smoothly as I once did. Looking at my hands, I have the proof. They're not as youthful as they once were. There are scars, healed burns and old stitch marks; all with a story or memory of how and when they got there. The *battles* that were waged with kitchen knives and hot ovens seem like just yesterday.

I thank God I found work that I truly enjoyed. It was a thrill for this kid from Indiana to come to California and have the dumb luck to survive in small business all these years. I am most grateful for those that gave me the breaks along the way.

I miss assembling the pieces of the puzzle of a new business; the *high* of working through a rush hour; The steaks and fish fillets grilling on open flames or the smell of hamburgers sizzling away and the printer buzzing away with new orders.

I have the fond memory of orchestrating meals…putting the plates together at precisely the right time and temperature and the camaraderie that I enjoyed with my *crews*. Thanks to the employees along the way who caught on fast and became stars to make my life a little easier. They also took pride in a job well done. It gets in your blood. For me, it wasn't all work. I had a lot of fun and laughs. I always managed to remember not to take myself too seriously. After all, it was just a job. I give thanks for the great and rewarding ride!

END

ABOUT THE AUTHOR

Randy Romack, was born and raised in Indianapolis, Indiana.. Growing up he attended P.S 21 on the south side of the inner city. Upon graduation from high school, he faced the reality of wading into an uncertain future with nothing more than the burning ambition to succeed. He tried his hand at a variety of jobs, but kept coming back to those related to the food industry. Throwing caution to the winds, he sought to abandon the cold Indiana winters, packed his meager possessions and moved to California, where he met a fellow meat cutter who shared his dream of wanting to own his own business

Together, they developed a formula that resulted in more than a dozen successful businesses. Randy eventually struck out on his own and developed several other successful restaurant concepts, among them Romack's Arrowhead Pizza & Delicatessen and Woody's Boathouse Restaurant.

He currently resides in Palm Desert, California with Dalva and Bella.

ACKNOWLEDGEMENTS

Nothing in life is more interesting than the people you meet along the way. I was fortunate to cross paths with many wonderful people and characters that influenced, amused fascinated and just down right entertained me. Thanks to those mentioned in this book. It sure was fun!

I would like to take this opportunity to express my gratitude and thank all of the people who gave me a break, supported me or just went along with some of my craziness while I was finding my way.

I must express my gratitude and love to my family for their understanding, self-sacrifices and willingness to forgive my obsession to pursue and fulfill my career dreams. Thanks for waiting so patiently for me.

Many thanks to Ron Sharrow, author of the Bruce West Novels, for sharing his tremendous writing skill, publishing know-how and help with the publication of this book

Thank you: David Landesman, Debra White and Dennis Wright.

Dalva
Eu sempre vou amar voce.

Made in the USA
Middletown, DE
18 February 2018